INTERIOR LANDSCAPES

Horticulture and Design

JEROME MALITZ AND SETH MALITZ

W. W. NORTON & COMPANY

New York • London

To Suzy, wife and mom

Also by Jerome Malitz:
Plants for the Future, a Gardener's Wishbook
Rocky Mountain National Park, a Dayhiker's Guide
Personal Landscapes
Introduction to Mathematical Logic

Authored jointly by Jerome and Seth Malitz:
Reflecting Nature, Garden Designs from Wild Landscapes

For information about permission to reproduce selections from this book,
write to Permissions, W. W. Norton & Company, Inc.,
500 Fifth Avenue, New Yotk, NY 10110

The text of this book is composed in Cochin
Manufacturing by KHL Printing Co Pte Ltd
Book design and composition by Gilda Hannah
Production manager: Leeann Graham

Library of Congress Cataloging-in-Publication Data
Malitz, Jerome, 1936–
Interior Landscapes: horticulture and design / Jerome Malitz and Seth Malitz.
p. cm.
Includes bibliographical references (p.) and index.
ISBN 0-393-73082-4
I. Interior landscaping. I. Malitz, Seth. II. Title.
SB419.25 .M35 2001   747'.98—dc21   2001044548

W. W. Norton & Company, Inc., 500 Fifth Avenue, New York, NY 10110
www.wwnorton.com
W.W. Norton & Company Ltd., Castle House, 75/76 Wells Street, London W1T 3QT

1 3 5 7 0 9 8 6 4 2

CONTENTS

Part I. The How and Why of Interior Landscapes   **5**

Chapter 1. Introduction   6

Chapter 2. Infrastructure   12

Chapter 3. Plants for the Purpose   22

Part II. From Places That Exist to Never-Never Lands:

      Examples of Interior Landscape Designs   **44**

Chapter 4. Fantasy Jungles   46

Chapter 5. Desert Geometry   74

Chapter 6. Dream Gardens   110

Chapter 7. Seasons   136

Chapter 8. Sanctuaries and Memorials   156

Chapter 9. Neither Here nor There   176

Part III. Drawings   **203**

Chapter 10. Things That Might Be   204

Sources for Tropical Plants and

      Horticultural Supplies   221

Bibliography   222

Plant Index   223

ACKNOWLEDGMENTS

Many thanks to the members of our No-name Horticulture Club. For years the members of this extraordinary group have been exchanging knowledge, enthusiasm, and plants—a more rabid bunch of "plant people" does not exist. We owe special thanks to the following members: Kevin Frender, who grows everything that can be grown and a few things that can't; Lloyd Gelman, staunch orchidist with a special passion for the cattleya alliance; Mark Haimes, hybridizer in search of more colorful and hardier magnolias; Paul Lembeck, orchidist and manager of Fantasy Orchids; Tom Lemieux, greenhouse manager and university lecturer on plants, taxonomy, and so much more; Shawn Quaely, landscaper, orchidist, and certified orchid judge; Jeff and Paula Shafer, cultivators and promoters of carnivorous plants; and Alan Taylor, expert on propagating and growing woody plants and not-so-woody plants. Our thanks also to Stan Gordon, owner of Fantasy Orchids, for his expert advice on many topics, and to Tim Mahoney, owner of Silver Mesa Cactus and Succulents, for expert advice on all things fleshy and thorny.

Most of all we want to thank Suzy Malitz, wife and mom. Our chief muse, critic, editor, and typist throughout the project, she silently suffered the sounds of construction, hysterical laughter, and uncontrolled shouting. She even tolerated our turning our entire house into a plant nursery. Nor did she complain (much) when we usurped the basement, garage, and patio for our gargantuan collection of wood, boulders, pebbles, gravel, and dirt. So, to Suzy—with all our love and gratitude—thanks.

PART ONE

The How and Why of Interior Landscapes

CHAPTER ONE

INTRODUCTION

eople love landscapes. They love them so much that they plan vacations around them, surround their homes with them, photograph them, paint pictures of them, and rhapsodize about them in poetry and song. So great is their love that seeing landscapes outdoors is not enough: They are driven to place them in public buildings, offices, and homes as well. Perhaps these indoor landscapes satisfy some need to make contact with nature. Maybe people marooned on islands of asphalt, concrete, steel, and glass crave some representation of nature—naturalistic, idealistic, or even abstract—that is close at hand, available in any season, in any climate, and at any time of the year.

An indoor landscape can be much more than a bit of décor. It can complement the architecture by harmony or contrast. It can change an ordinary interior into something quite extraordinary, something that captures your spirit and gives your imagination wings.

A landscape in a building can free you of the walls. Alive with exotic plants from the equatorial rain-

forests, an atrium can transport you deep into a jungle, but without the fear of leeches and cobras. Make an enclosure perpetually cool and dripping with moisture, fill it with strange and wonderful orchids, ferns, and mosses, and let your mind wander through the world's tropical highlands. Or perhaps you prefer a garden that mirrors the driest regions of the world, a garden filled with bizarre and beautiful succulents, weirdly shaped rocks, twisted wood, and colored sand—a desert garden you can visit without want of water or fear of scorpions.

Maybe the landscapes you prefer are more abstract, have fewer plants, or even none at all. Perhaps the austere grandeur of a place like Utah's Arches National Park is what moves you most of all. Maybe your favorite kind of environment has more sculptural structure, a geometrical or architectural appearance. If you prefer to see more of the human hand and mind in the interpretation, you might prefer the aesthetics of a sculpture court or the meditative tranquility of a Zen Buddhist dry garden. An interior landscape can evoke any of these

environments convincingly and powerfully.

We admit to loving all of these types of landscapes with equal passion. But we are not purists, and we even enjoy landscapes that mix and match various elements, juxtaposing industrial forms and materials with those that come from nature. In fact, we are greatly confused as to the differences, and we want to stay that way. We can easily distinguish between abstract and naturalistic designs when presented with examples near the ends of the continuum, but the demarcation between the two seems obscure. Is Arches National Park naturalistic? Supposedly it is, as it is entirely the work of nature. On the other hand, many of the park's forms—cylinders, cones, parallelepipeds—are so geometric that they can be classified mathematically. And what of the Zen Buddhist stone gardens in China and Japan? They are abstract to an extreme but are also clearly representational, as they were planned to be. It is this delicious confusion that we find so fascinating and that we often try to express in our designs.

What is an interior landscape? Defining it would limit it, and that we do not want to do. Besides, a rigorous definition is impossible. In our view, however, an interior landscape is any indoor construction or arrangement that calls to mind landscapes of nature or outdoor gardens. The construction need not be a slavish copy or miniaturization of an outdoor model but instead can reflect its inspiration abstractly, indirectly, and with artistic license. Even a single potted tree could be considered an interior landscape, although a profoundly boring one of little inspiration.

What Pleases Us

The interior landscapes that we are interested in are those that are strongly expressive, connect with our emotions, and communicate a sense of place. We prefer pieces with a strong sculptural component and pieces that are an integral part of their architectural setting rather than merely a pretty, incidental tack-on.

Usually complexity engages us more than simplicity. We are not minimalists by nature. Complexity feeds interest; simplicity often thwarts it. After all, if one glance from one viewpoint is enough to establish the design in the mind, why bother to explore the piece in its entirety? It would be a waste of time. However, the danger in complexity is confusion, and incoherently juxtaposing too many elements also results in boredom. The challenge, then, is this: to make a design rich enough in its visual elements and allusions to sustain interest but organized enough so as not to confuse the observer with too much detail.

How can this be accomplished? By organizing the parts within the whole. A symphony is organized like this: themes are arranged into passages, passages into movements, movements into an entire work. In a visual design, various sections can have their own appeal, while larger passages organize them into something with a different effect. Meanwhile, the piece as a whole can communicate something else again.

On the other hand, simplicity may serve best if the design must have an instant impact, especially if it is to be seen only occasionally or in passing. And there are other arguments for simplicity. If the design is to convey a sense of monumentality, timelessness, or solemnity, directness and simplicity may be the best choices. Serenity in a design also may be best achieved by simplicity. And a simple approach may be the best one to encourage introspection and contemplation.

We appreciate novelty, but not as an end in itself. Interior landscape designs should not grandstand or serve the ego or establish an identity for the designer. Rather, novelty should be used to bring new insight to the potential of design; to explore the power of landscapes to affect our emotions, sensibilities, and awareness; to extend the capability of the art and craft of landscape design. Novelty for novelty's sake is ultimately pointless and boring. Of course, a piece totally devoid of novelty can be just as boring.

It should be noted that novelty does not pertain solely to a design's conceptual basis and visual impact; a piece can have other aspects that are novel. For example, the materials and techniques of construction might be new. In pieces using plants, the methods of maintenance and the plants themselves might be new to the application. But these are technical concerns and may be of more interest to the designer than to the observer.

Finally, we admire work that respects its surroundings: work that fits into its architectural setting, that complements it and is complemented by it. How outrageously self-serving and arrogant for designers to show off their creativity by designing a piece that upstages its surroundings! A more honest test of the designer's skill is to create a landscape that honors its surroundings.

In the Eyes of the Beholder

Why mention the things we look for in a landscape? Because they are what concern us when we design our own landscapes. Because we hope that others will agree with us on what criteria should be used to judge a design and that what pleases us will also please some of them. Otherwise, what is the point of creating anything? If there were no possibility of communicating with others through art or music or landscape design, why would anyone bother to paint, compose, or design a landscape? Is beauty solely in the eyes of the beholder? We hope not. What a pity if it were—then we would really be a lonely species.

Of course, culture and experience influence taste in art, music, and design, and in some instances completely determine them. But as members of the same species, we respond to a great number of stimuli in the same way. We believe these responses are instinctive and not easily modified. Perhaps it is through these common responses that we are able to communicate by means of art, music, and design.

Dissonance can be quantified. Certain chords, timbres, and tones are soothing; others agitate. Certain rhythms calm us; others arouse anxiety. We describe pure tones as cold; others that are well nuanced with overtones as warm. Is there someone who doesn't cringe when fingernails are scratched across a blackboard? And when listening to music we await the return to the tonic; when it isn't forthcoming, we are on edge. Mozart is rumored to have fainted dead away upon hearing a dissonant chord—bless his exquisite sensibilities! Enough discordance makes even the leaden-eared wince.

Our responses to certain visual stimuli also point to the similarities of our hard-wiring. The same optical illusions fool everyone's eyes: The length of a two-headed arrow shrinks when the arrows point outward and expands when the arrows point inward. M. C. Escher gives us vertigo when his drawings of staircases double back on themselves in an ever-descending/ascending Möbius strip. The op artist Bridget Riley assaults our optic pathways to the point of nausea and migraine, and no one seems to be immune.

The conclusion seems inescapable: We are all hard-wired in a similar fashion. At first this might seem upsetting, an assault on our individuality and self-determination. Of course, some of our perceptions and responses are tempered and determined by our culture and experience. But many of our most basic responses are hard to modify and play an important role in our appreciation of art, music, and design. We believe that nonverbal communication is based on such shared common responses. Exactly how remains a mystery: The effects are too complicated to be scientifically understood, at least for now. And this leaves the wonder and magic of nonverbal communication through the arts quite intact.

In Search of the Muse

The examples in part II of this book are of our own design. But nothing is created in a vacuum; our work reflects many influences. Sculpture, painting, and architecture have all played a role. We have learned a great deal about color, spatial organization, and the use of materials from these disciplines.

Outdoor gardens—traditional and modern, abstract and representational—certainly have had an influence. Although we admit to having favorites, we have tried to remain open to all forms and to find in each garden that we see both its strong points and its weak points. A camera and a tripod help us to sort out the details and focus our attention while providing a crutch for our memory.

But our greatest source of ideas is nature. Hiking wilderness trails along beaches, deserts, and forests provides more inspiration than one can ever use. The greatest landscapes are out there, and it's ultimately there that each of us learns to love them. As always, a camera is with us.

We wish we could be more explicit in describing our influences, but there are too many of them, and they have become too amalgamated in our minds to be sorted out. But the confusion is a blessing, and we continue to gather materials and ideas to add to it.

A Landscape Design From Scratch

How do we go about designing a landscape? In fits and starts. The process we follow is as varied as our sources of inspiration and as changeable as our intentions, goals, and moods.

We may decide in advance on a theme or direction. Perhaps a memory of a photograph triggers the idea. We then may hunt for that photograph and others that might be of use. We may search through our files of drawings for something that is relevant. We may make a new series of drawings, cranking out as many as we can, with as much variation as possible. We may build small-scale models to work out the three-dimensional aspect of the design, again with as many variations as we can come up with. The process continues and steps are repeated until we see that nothing more is to be gained.

Then comes the first of many reality checks: What materials are needed? Do we have them or can we get them? What are the demands on space? How difficult will it be to set up the piece? How much time will be required? Only when all of these questions and more yield favorable answers do we continue.

With some mental image of where we want to go, and some idea of how to get there, we start putting together the infrastructure of the design. We may have to construct certain components specifically for the project, or we may have to go out and beg for, borrow, or buy the materials. Usually most of the things we need are already at hand.

We are confirmed packrats, and we have been collecting all sorts of stuff over dozens of years. Piles of driftwood, slabs of stone, rocks from pea size to basketball size, gravel, and pots and potting materials of all sorts are only part of the clutter. We haven't used all of it, and we never will. But these things are often of interest in themselves, and playing with them, pushing them around, and arranging them helps us get to know them—not just their shape and color, but also their spirit, their energy, and how they get along with each other. We get to know them personally. This process is not only good sport but also has led to many ideas for landscapes. Sometimes these ideas are richer and more complex than any we can generate using drawings or photographs alone.

When the infrastructure is finished, the piece may be finished— some of our landscapes do not use living plants at all. If plants are called for, we take them from our own collection. Their final arrangement is seldom worked out in advance. We shove them around until we think the composition works as well as it is going to work.

Then it is time for a break. But for the next several days or weeks, we continue to make adjustments and alterations until we finally decide that enough is enough.

Yet to Come

This book is divided into ten chapters, the first three of which deal with the practical aspects of designing and maintaining an interior landscape. The remaining chapters consist of a portfolio of examples of our own designs. A color photograph illustrates each example, and an essay describes the effect we set out to obtain and the methods and materials we used to achieve it. The essay evaluates the approach on aesthetic and practical grounds. We stress that this is both a "how-to" book as well as a sourcebook for interior landscape design ideas.

The second chapter, "Infrastructure," describes the inorganic materials we use to create the landscapes —where we obtain the real rock, wood, stones and gravel, as well as how their artificial counterparts are manufactured.

Plants for interior landscapes must be chosen with great care. Light, water, and humidity requirements, potting needs, rate of growth, pruning demands, freedom from pests and diseases, longevity, size, and obtainability are some of the factors that must be considered. Of course, a plant's appearance is a major consideration, especially when it is part of an ensemble. Chapter 3, "Plants for the Purpose," gives a critical description of the most useful plants available for interior landscaping. Both their merits and their faults are discussed, and many are grouped in photographs. This, along with the many images showing the plants in our interior landscapes, provides a useful guide not only for those who wish to incorporate the plants into landscapes of their own, but also for those who wish to enjoy a collection of exotic plants in their homes or offices in a less structured setting.

Chapter 4, "Fantasy Jungles," gives glimpses into corners of an idealized tropical jungle, places where morpho butterflies or birds of paradise might feel at home. One

can find orchids both bizarre and beautiful, begonias with leaves of satin brocade, patent leather alocasias, bromeliads of tortoiseshell and jade, and all sorts of other strange and wonderful plants. But it is the overall composition rather than the individual plants that establishes the exotic mood.

The landscapes in chapter 5, "Desert Geometry," were inspired by drylands—arid regions of the world where stone, sand, cacti, and other succulents create an abstract geometry that seems more akin to modern sculpture than to other landscapes. We explore this theme with a variety of pieces, some naturalistic and others quite abstract.

Welcome to the scented garden, where the fragrance of gardenias fills the air. Welcome to the moonlit garden, where white moth orchids float on stems so slender they are almost invisible. Welcome to the hanging garden, where epiphytic staghorn ferns display their antlers, carnivorous nepenthes dangle their deadly pitchers, and Spanish moss festoons the branches. In these indoor gardens described in chapter 6, "Dream

Gardens," space is layered into successive planes by split walls, gates, and trellises. These features magnify depth and evoke a sense of mystery as the mind wanders through the design in search of what lies beyond the next plane. These are gardens meant for dreaming.

In the temperate regions of the world, each season bestows its own special splendor on the landscape. Each act of this annual four-act play is scripted to be as different from the others as possible. Although spring and fall are also represented in chapter 7, "Seasons," we have placed special emphasis on winter. It's a time we particularly love—a time when cold, ice, and snow chisel away the superfluous, revealing the landscape's essential structure in all its serene purity. Summer is not

included because many of the pieces in chapter 4 and 6 can be interpreted as such.

Chapter 8, "Sanctuaries and Memorials," offers quiet pieces, pieces that invite meditation. The plan of most is simple, almost somber, evocative but explicit. Some designs are so concise they are scale-independent: They can be realized in the confines of a small room or span a space several stories high. They can be private and intimate or public and heroic in size. All of these landscapes are intended to turn viewers' thoughts inward, even as their attention is drawn into the scene.

Chapter 9, "Neither Here nor There," presents a miscellany of pieces that, because of theme or style, do not fit easily into the other chapters. Some of the more painter-

ly pieces explore the possibility of using strong color as a major component of the design. Others come closer to abstract sculpture. A few designs are whimsical, leaning toward humor in some cases, pure kitsch in others. All of these pieces suggest new directions to explore in the future.

Many of our designs exist only as drawings. Some of the designs are unrealistically ambitious, but others are eminently doable, and even the more fanciful designs may have the germ of a usable idea. Chapter 10 offers a small sample of these sketches, if for no other reason than to show how we generate a landscape design.

❋ ❋ ❋

This book is for people who design interior landscapes professionally,

as well as for those who do it for their own pleasure. It's for those whose passion is plants and who want to display their darlings to the very best effect. It is for those involved in the blood sport of growing the difficult and flowering the impossible and who want a stage to show off their prowess. But most of all, this book is for individuals who love landscapes—wilderness landscapes, interior landscapes, and landscapes of the mind.

Interior landscaping is a hybrid activity: part sculpture, part architectural design, and part gardening. It can be far more than mere decoration. It can speak to you poetically, alter your mood, and spark your imagination. Interior landscapes—and the pleasure they can bring—have no limits.

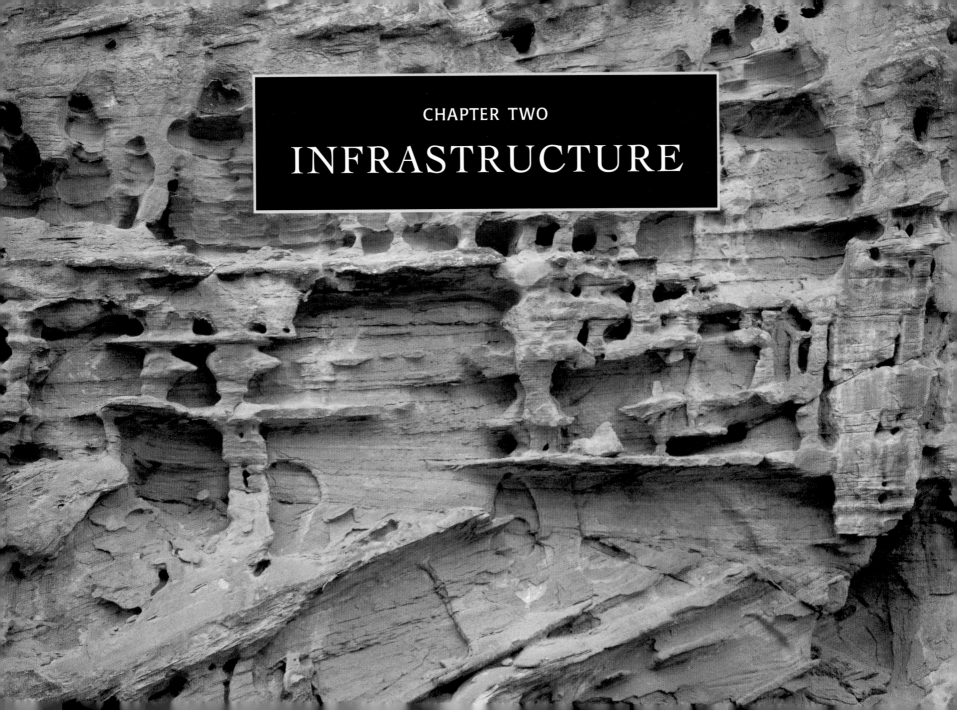

CHAPTER TWO

INFRASTRUCTURE

There is more to a landscape than just its plants —stone formations, water features, and the lay of the land can all play a part. Even in landscapes where plants are a dominant feature, the nonliving components form a stage that sets them off perfectly, providing contrast in color, texture, and form. Although most of our designs employ both living and nonliving elements, there are some that have no plants at all—their effect depends entirely on nonliving components.

"Dry landscapes" of only rock and gravel were designed by Buddhist monks in China and Japan more than eight hundred years ago, and some of them survive today, essentially unchanged. Tray landscapes, in which stones are arranged on a flat stone tray to suggest mountain ranges, canyons, or coastal scenery, have been treasured in both countries for centuries. Designing such landscapes is considered a high art, and there is no denying the inventiveness needed to create such a diversity of designs from such limited resources. More modern versions of plantless landscapes can be found as sculpture courts worldwide. Those that feature abstract stone sculpture almost seem like tray landscapes magnified to a monumental scale.

In nature, there are many magnificent landscapes in which plants play no role whatsoever, or play such a minor role that they are easily overlooked. You see such landscapes in the regions of perpetual snow and ice, in the Arctic and in the high alpine reaches of the world. You see them in the deserts —in Bryce, Zion, Grand Canyon, Arches, Capitol Reef, and Canyonlands National Parks, to name just a few in North America alone. And you see them on the coasts of every continent, wherever the ocean sculpts the rocky shores.

Even if plants do play a major role during the growing season, a landscape still may have much to offer during the dormant season. Many of the classic gardens of China are like this. These gardens were designed to celebrate the seasons by emphasizing the distinctive beauty that each has to offer. It's a design philosophy that we miss in certain flower gardens, where the end of the season robs them of any interest until the following spring.

In our own landscapes, far from wanting to cover the infrastructure under a mantle of plants, we leave as much of it exposed as is consistent with the design. In some of our pieces the infrastructure is everything; in others, its role is less obvious.

What kind of infrastructure is needed for an interior landscape? What materials are suitable? There are absolutely no restrictions that we know of. Different designers choose different materials, and the choices reflect such mundane concerns as cost, availability, and the ease and safety with which they can be worked. The appearance of the material and its contribution to the entire design may be the first concern.

In this chapter we describe some of the nonliving materials we use in our designs. New materials and new ways of working with the old ones are being invented all the time, and it is not easy to keep up with it all. But this is what makes these times so exciting for the designer—the prospect of using new methods and materials to facilitate the passage from the imagined design to its realization.

Most of the materials we use in our interior landscapes are used often in outdoor landscapes: driftwood, stone (both artificial and natural), different kinds of gravel, and wood (both machined and raw). Also mentioned are some of the materials we have worked with less frequently but expect to use more in the future: cloth, plastic, tile, and ceramics. Additionally, we will describe some of the backgrounds that we used. Some were fortuitous finds, but others we constructed, and we will explain how that was done. But before we do this, let's consider the installation site.

On Site

The designer seldom has complete freedom to choose the size of the landscape and the materials used in its construction. The intended site of the installation imposes restrictions on both. And it is usual-

---

2-1 Dry interior landscape in the Sussex Building, Boulder, Colorado

ly more efficient in terms of cost, time, and energy to adapt the design rather than to rework the site.

The weight-bearing capacity of the floors and walls of the installation site must be the primary consideration in the choice of materials. Unfortunately, the exact weight-bearing capacity can seldom be determined and the best that one can hope for is a conservative estimation by a structural engineer. The best rule of thumb is simply to make the piece as light as possible. This is where knowledge of alternative materials and construction methods is important.

A superb interior landscape in the Sussex Building in Boulder, Colorado, is an exception to the rule (figure 2-1). It stretches fully half the length of the first floor—perhaps 60 ft (18 m) or more. The inspiration of Kanjuro Shibata, a twentieth-generation bow maker to the emperor of Japan, it is a modern masterpiece in the Zen Buddhist dry-landscape style. There are no plants and no water, although all sorts of water features are strongly suggested: A "waterfall" tumbles down a distant mountain and gathers to form the headwaters of a "stream," which meanders through the length of the composition, occasionally widening into a pond and then narrowing to flow under a bridge.

The designer wanted to use real rock and gravel in the composition, but as the piece took shape and more and more rock was brought in, it became obvious that the floor was not likely to support all of that weight. Rather than compromise the design, additional joists and pillars were installed in the basement parking structure beneath the floor. Such retrofitting is a logistical nightmare and involves a great amount of time and money. But here the strategy worked, and the floor shows no sign of stress either from above or below.

The designer of this landscape was probably committed to the use of authentic natural materials for philosophical reasons. But designers not bound by such convictions should give some thought to using artificial substitutes for such heavy materials—substitutes that are lightweight and easy to install. Artificial rocks, trees, and gravel can be fabricated with enough realism to get past anyone who doesn't give them the thump test. And such a strategy might save enough time, money, and energy to assuage the conscience of all but the most rabid purists. (The materials and techniques that can be used as Mother Nature substitutes are discussed later.)

The second major consideration is electricity—an interior landscape almost certainly will require it. With a bit of electricity under your command, you get to play God, controlling the light and the climate, at least locally. Even if there are no living plants, it is unlikely that normal room lighting will present the piece at its best. The direction won't be quite what you want and consequently the shadows won't be quite right. The color might be off or too flat, and the intensity inappropriate. For these reasons, proper lighting must be installed.

The task is much more complicated if the landscape has living plants, and the designer must be willing to compromise. If the plants require intense light, soft shadows may have to be sacrificed. Give these plants subdued light, and they will elongate, stretching into a lanky, sprawling mess. Setting the lights off to one side might give you more dramatic shadows and emphasize the contours of the design. But then phototropism (attraction toward light) will have the plants bowing to a nonexistent audience in the wings. Change the diurnal rhythm (lights on for so many hours, off for so many hours), and plants that you expect to flower will refuse to do so. (It is strange that plants from the tropics near the equator should be influenced by day length!) And plants that need a bit of dormancy for a few months in order to grow and bloom properly might do neither without the appropriate cues from the light.

Even with the light's intensity and diurnal schedule properly worked out, you might have to worry about the quality of the light: Is the spectrum what it should be to promote blooming (if that is important) and adequate growth? Not so long ago, lights designed for this purpose had peaks in the red and blue range of their spectrum, and the light they delivered was garish and unnatural—just plain ugly to most viewers. But now there are all sorts of lightbulbs—incandescent, fluorescent, halogen, sodium vapor —that promote both blooming and growth with a spectrum that is so close to that of daylight you will not notice a difference.

With electricity to do your bidding, you can also customize the climate. Controlling temperature is no problem whatsoever. Small heating units of various designs will bring desert heat to your cacti and succulents or jungle heat to your tropicals. You can even install miniature cooling systems to create highland temperatures, should you want to grow orchids from the Andes.

Of course, there is a difference between jungle heat and desert heat—between a muggy New York summer heat and a parched, dry Arizona heat. But with a bit of electricity, you can mimic either. Small humidifiers and dehumidifiers run for pennies a day and will give you just the degree of air moisture your plants need. There are even foggers and misters that will put on a bit of a show when delivering the humidity. Often they are connected to timers so that a blanket of fog will roll in and roll out right on schedule.

Water can play an even more prominent role in the landscape. Miniature pumps will give you a cascade, a stream, or even a waterfall. It's all possible with a current of electricity at your command.

Materials

After the site is chosen and evaluated, the designer can turn to the construction of the piece itself. What is needed in a particular application depends on the design and the designer, but a few staples will serve any designer well.

Backgrounds

Some setups don't need them, some can't have them. If the piece is meant to be seen from all sides, then the background is what you happen to see when you look through the arrangement to the other side. Exactly what you see changes as you change your position. If the piece is set against a wall, the wall can be your background, as long as its materials—brick, stone, wood paneling, painted wallboard, etc.—provide the color and texture you want. Or the piece can be set against a window; if the window looks out onto some nice bit of scenery or the sky, then you have your background.

In most cases, however, the background that comes with the site is not what is needed. This gives you the opportunity to construct the background yourself. There are many ways to do this: Piecing together boards of wood, tree bark (including cork), flat sheets of stone, or even mirrors or aluminum panels will work, and each will have an application in which it is best suited.

We have recently begun working with panels of Masonite, which offer more control and flexibility. (Most of the pieces pictured in this book have Masonite backgrounds.) We first made each panel more rigid by gluing furring strips to its back (rough) side. The smooth side was then sanded lightly to give more tooth for better paint adhesion. This side and all edges were then carefully painted with several coats of acrylic gesso for protection from moisture and to further prepare the surface to receive the additional layers. Next a latex wall texture was spread over the panel and then sculpted into a low-relief pattern simulating mud or rock. Ideas for the patterns were found in nature—a mud wall in Capitol Reef National Park, Utah (figure 2-2); pot rock and lacerock typical of Capitol Reef and Arches National Parks, Utah, and Larrabee State Park, Washington (figure 2-3); schist from Maligne Canyon in Jasper National Park, Canada (figure 2-4); and other more exotic sources. The texture was then given multiple layers of flat acrylic paint. At no time did we feel obliged to slavishly copy the model; rather, we interpreted the original in whatever way seemed appropriate (see figures 4-15, 5-6, and 9-3). The panels have proved to be remarkably durable and easy to repair. We do not know how well they will hold up in the long run, but they show no deterioration over two years of use. Another advantage to using panels is that they can be disassociated and staggered or combined with others

2-3 Lacerock wall, Arches National Park, Utah

2-2 Canyon wall, Capitol Reef National Park, Utah

(see figures 5-3, 8-1, and 8-7). This greatly expands their design applications.

There are many other techniques that can be used to make backgrounds. Cement or plaster can be sculpted in place over metal mesh, or slabs of Styrofoam can be sculpted with a hot soldering iron. The background can be carved out of wood, hammered out of copper sheet, tiled out of random flat pieces of rock, or modeled out of clay. These are just some of the possibilities.

Wood

Once we were collecting downed wood in an old cottonwood forest and had assembled quite a pile when a stranger walking his dog stopped to assess the project. His first quick glance led him to comment, "What beautiful wood." But after his second glance, which

2-4 Canyon wall with waterfall, Maligne Canyon, Jasper National Park, Canada

caused him to screw up his face in pain, he decided, "Well, at least it's full of character." That is exactly the kind of wood we look for: wind-twisted, age-bent, well-noshed by fungus and bugs—character pieces. This wood captures our eye, sustains our interest, and proves most useful in the setups, without stealing the scene from the other elements of the design by being overly pretty. And once in place, it gives the arrangement the appearance of age (it's been there long enough for the wood to rot), while simultaneously conveying a dynamic quality (it's rotting). Rotten, misshapen wood has another virtue: Fragments can be pieced together seamlessly into larger shapes, which permits more sculptural license (see figures 5-6 and 6-1).

Such wood, however, is unlikely to hold up to the tropical or sub-tropical climate of many interior landscapes. For these applications we coat the wood with a clear polyester or urethane finish. Dipping is often a more efficient method of applying the plastic than painting. Wood that has been treated in this way holds up quite well, even under terrarium conditions. In fact, the more porous the wood, the more efficiently it takes up the plastic, and the stronger the result. If still more strength and permanence is needed, the wood can be coated with epoxy. But different coatings and different woods interact differently. We have learned this the hard way, through many unpleasant surprises. So always run a test on an expendable piece.

Artificial root forms, branches, and entire trees can be fashioned out of an epoxy-based, spreadable paste: An armature of rebar is covered with one-eighth–in (about three mm) mesh hardware cloth, and the epoxy paste is troweled over the screen. The technique has had wide applications in furnishing zoo enclosures (see *Time*, June 28, 1999, pages 50–51 for a photograph of a large installation in a gorilla compound).

The same basic idea can be varied with less expensive and more easily obtained materials. Again starting with a rebar armature, one can apply fiberglass in place of epoxy paste and hardware cloth. Alternatively, strips of cloth mesh impregnated with plaster of paris will work. All of this is messy, time-consuming work.

Artificial wood (crafted out of ceramic) is widely used to furnish aquariums and terrariums and is available from pet stores. Some of this material is quite convincing. Of course, small pieces can be glued together to form larger structures.

Stone

Stone is a key component of many landscapes, natural and manmade, outdoors and indoors. It establishes a ruggedness and permanence that is hard to achieve with any other material, and it is a perfect foil for plants, setting them off by contrast in color, texture, and form. Even used alone, as in the "dry landscape" tradition of China and Japan, stone

Stone Recipe

1. Mix 1 part Portland cement to 2-3 parts horticultural perlite. If the piece that you are making requires additional strength, you can add glass fiber or cement fortifier, both of which are available at most hardware stores.

2. Add 1 part water and cement dye (also available at most hardware stores), and mix together.

The finished mixture can be worked for more than an hour as it gradually stiffens. Embedding hardware cloth or an armature into the form increases the strength. Even a piece an inch (2.5 cm) thick takes days to cure.

can communicate the majesty of a mountain range or a rocky coast.

There is an endless variety of stone that can be used in landscape design. Natural stone is available in every imaginable color, form, and texture, as well as in many that can't be imagined. Even slate, most commonly seen as a dark gray sheet, can be found in a vast array of colors and patterns. And rock is available in limitless forms—thin sheets, heavy slabs, quarried cubes, and freeform boulders from pebble size to Volkswagen size and beyond. Sandstone, limestone, granite, and marble are commonly available in all of these forms.

One of our favorite stones is lacerock (sometimes called "pot rock"). It is often found in fluted sheets that appear to be much heavier and more massive than they actually are unless you view them along an edge. Lacerock is used as landscape rock and in aquariums and is available from stoneyards and pet shops. Sheets of lacerock have distinctively different sides. On one side the rock is relatively smooth; in color and texture it resembles roughly troweled concrete. The other side is highly ornamented with pits, holes, and ridges. We find both sides useful: In figures 5-4 and 5-5 the rough side is utilized; in figures 5-14 and 5-16 it is the smooth side.

Natural stone can be customized to suit the application. Stone can be shaped by chipping, cutting, and abrading. Smaller pieces can be assembled into larger ones by the use of mortar or a variety of glues (epoxy-based glues are particularly strong and durable). However, shaping natural stone is usually a difficult, time-consuming, dirty task and often requires considerable skill and experience. Some stone, such as granite and lacerock, are exceedingly difficult to shape. Tough and strong-willed, they strongly resist the saw and chisel, and when they do yield it is often on their terms—fissuring and cracking as they see fit. So it is usually best to accept them and work with them in their original shape.

There are several other major drawbacks to using natural stone. Acceptable stone may not be available locally, and having it shipped to you sight unseen is not only expensive but also risky—a piece that is entirely the wrong color or shape may end up sitting paid for and delivered at the site. The weight of real stone also is an important consideration. Installing a large setup using stone may require heavy machinery and careful assessment of risk to people and property.

Thus, it is often prudent to forego the use of natural stone in favor of artificial stone. There are several different ways of constructing and customizing artificial stone. From the Bronx Zoo to the Los Angeles County Zoo, from the Denver Zoo to the Arizona-Sonora Desert Museum, examples of artificial stone the size of apartment buildings are realistic enough to fool the zoo's inhabitants and most of the visitors (figure 2-5).

There are many ways of constructing artificial stone, and the most common methods use concrete. Small forms can be cast as a solid mass in molds made out of wax, clay, plaster of paris, and all sorts of other materials. The recipe on the left makes a strong but light concrete that is one-third the weight of the usual mix based on cement, sand, and gravel.

Larger structures can be fashioned by troweling or blowing a concrete mix over hardware cloth fastened to an armature of rebar. Alternatively, the concrete can be spread over a polystyrene or Styrofoam core. The

2-5 Artificial rock canyon, Arizona-Sonora Desert Museum, Tucson, Arizona. The tree is an Arizona sycamore (*Platanus wrightii*).

concrete can be modeled while setting up and later its surface can be painted with acrylic or epoxy paint.

The Denver Zoo has enormous installations of fake rock constructed out of panels cast in latex rubber molds that were taken from actual stone outcroppings. Some of these exhibits have been in place for more than half a century and seem to improve in appearance and become more convincing with each passing year.

The general fabrication methods used for concrete can also be used with other materials. Artificial stone can be fashioned out of fiberglass draped on an armature or foam core. Alternatively, an epoxy-based modeling paste can be spread over eighth-inch mesh hardware cloth supported by a rebar frame in much the same way that concrete ones are created. These plastic rocks are much lighter and tougher than those fashioned from concrete, even the lightweight mix. Wood and plaster can also be made to look like stone with a coating of acrylic or, preferably, epoxy paint.

Ground Covers

In addition to ease of maintenance and the visual contribution to the design, the structural constraints of the installation site should be considered when a ground cover is being chosen. A large installation using granite gravel to a depth of 4 in (10 cm) places far more stress on the floor than our artificial gravel, scoria, or expanded clay pellets. Even the water-holding capacity of the material should be considered: For example, bark mulch, which is light when dry, can be quite heavy when wet, and silica sand, already heavy when dry, is nearly fifty percent heavier when wet.

Although we occasionally use organic ground covers such as bark mulch, we prefer inorganic materials, as they allow a wide choice of

Gravel Recipe

We use the same mixture as we do for artificial rock (except that dye is not always needed). Perlite is available in several grades—fine to coarse—and this allows us to control granularity. No glass fiber or cement fortifier is used. But there are differences in the way the material is handled.

1. After mixing, spread out mixture to a thickness of one inch or less.

2. For the first twelve hours, turn, break up, and respread the material every four hours.

3. Allow two days for the gravel to cure.

4. Sift out the fine particles through a strainer and then wash the gravel in a box with a screen bottom.

color and texture. Washed, the inorganic material is cleaner, more stable, and less likely to harbor unwanted creatures. Because the terrestrial plants that we use in our designs are in pots, the merit of the ground cover as a growing medium is of no concern—inert sand or gravel is as good as rich soil. The pots are sunk into the ground cover and topped with the material. Pet stores that cater to the tropical fish trade usually carry packaged sand and gravel for use in aquariums. Some of this material is natural and looks natural, but some of it is coated with epoxy paint in eye-bashing colors. Usually packaged in small quantities for aquarists, the price is steep.

Commercial gravel companies that serve the building industry and landscapers usually stock a variety of gravels. Even road base (squeegee) and pea gravel can be useful; chipped and crushed rock may be less so. Red and black scoria in pea-gravel grade or finer is light and well suited for desert landscapes indoors or outdoors. Horticultural supply firms offer clay pellets, fired and filled with air pockets, in a wide variety of sizes and earth tones. They are a light, clean material that is easy to work with. There are many other suitable ground covers that you can find in all sorts of places if you are willing to explore.

Gravel can also be homemade—doing so not only saves money, but also allows you to get the exact texture, granularity, and color that you want. Furthermore, fake gravel weighs about a third of the weight of real gravel.

Concrete as Concrete

In several of our pieces, concrete is used as concrete—we do not attempt to disguise it as natural stone or some other material. Usually the forms are rectilinear and the color is pale gray or tan. Used in this way, concrete lends a strong sculptural and architectural aspect to a design while providing a strong counterpoint for plants.

Concrete slabs and blocks are available in various sizes at lumber stores and garden centers. Mortar can be used to join pieces together into larger structures. More complicated shapes can be cast from molds made of wood, sheet metal, clay (artificial or natural), modeling wax, and other materials. But the weight of concrete should always be taken into account.

There are several different approaches that can be used to keep the weight down. The recipe for artificial rock given earlier reduces the weight by two thirds. Other strategies for producing fake rock previously mentioned can be used to make large but light concrete forms: Hardware cloth or special screening designed to hold concrete can be fastened to an armature made of welded rebar or welded angle iron. Then a slurry of concrete, often with an addition of lime, is sprayed or troweled onto the screen. Alternatively, such a slurry can be worked over a solid Styrofoam or polystyrene form, or sand and gravel can be mixed with epoxy to produce an extremely durable, inert "concrete" that can be spread over wire mesh in a very thin layer. All of these techniques minimize weight.

Concrete and epoxy-sand mixes are fairly inert once they have cured. However, lime in concrete can leach out in a moist environment and make the soil unsuitable for plants. In this situation a barrier paint, available in building supply centers, lumberyards, and most hardware stores, can be used to seal the limed concrete.

Paint

Occasionally the color of some component of the infrastructure must be adjusted. What kind of paint should be used? It depends on what is being painted and the permanence that is required. In an indoor application, the moisture in the surroundings, not ultraviolet radiation, determines the longevity of the paint.

Acrylic latex-based paints are convenient to use and fairly durable. Oil paints are somewhat less convenient, but they are more durable under moist conditions. The glossier the finish, the more durable the surface is, but a glossy finish might not be appropriate for the design. Urethane-based boat paints designed for use above waterline are even more durable but even less convenient to apply. (Paints formulated for application below the waterline contain copper designed to gradually slough off. This prevents marine organisms from fouling the hull. But copper in high concentrations is lethal to plants.)

Another alternative is epoxy paint. This is the most durable of all, but by far the most expensive and least convenient. It is not widely available, and special colors must be prepared for the application at hand.

A number of different paints are designed to inhibit or prevent moisture from passing across a concrete barrier, and they can be explored as the need arises. Other specialized applications should be researched carefully. For example, the use of metallic coatings is an exciting possibility but a potential hazard to plants. A metallic paint with an epoxy base is likely to be a good choice. Automobile lacquers are a fine choice but need to be oven cured. Metal plating is another interesting possibility. In short, there are many surface treatments that can be explored.

Fake Plants

Yes, it's true. Sometimes we use fake plants. Mentioning them here stretches the notion of infrastructure a bit, but when we use them it is always as an underlying design component and never as a point of independent interest.

Although some purists may con-sider it a sneaky subterfuge, using fake plants works quite well in certain situations. Fake plants can be used when a plant of a certain size or shape is needed but is not available. A fake plant can be placed in light too dim to support a live plant, so close to the light that a live plant would be fried, or so far out of reach that a live plant would starve. If a fake plant doesn't have exactly the right shape, it can be further faked through pruning; furthermore, you can prune it to any required shape and it will take no offense and show no signs of distress. Always ready to do service, fake plants are easy keepers and take no umbrage at any amount of neglect.

That's the trouble with them. They are such stalwarts—so reliable, so unchanging, so unchallenging—as to be really boring. But our main concern is the integrity of the overall design, and not the interest of the individual components. If a fake plant serves the design best, it should be used unapologetically. Still, whenever we use a fake plant, we suffer pangs of conscience.

Our favorite fake is *Ficus fakius* (binomial courtesy of our friend Kevin Frender, plantsman extraordinaire). Stand back a couple of feet, and it looks exactly like the common indoor fig tree *Ficus benjamina* (see figures 4-9, 6-9, and 6-12). Our other favorite fake is something we custom-make ourselves: fake moss or *Selaginella*, or *Mossus fakius* as we affectionately call it (see figures 6-6, 6-7, and 9-2). We take real sea sponges and slice them with a knife into cushionlike shapes. They then are soaked in thinned, gray-green acrylic paint, dried, and highlighted with yellow-green. There you have it—animal into plant. It works well enough for us to extend the effect of true moss or *Selaginella* into places where it cannot grow.

Other Additions

There are other components that we use in the infrastructure of the setups. Inverted pots, tubes and pipes of rigid plastic, nylon fishing line, polycord, wire of various gauges, concrete blocks—the list goes on and on. Most of these devices are used to elevate or stabi-lize the plants, wood, and rocks. But in many cases these materials are visually interesting in and of themselves; for instance, concrete blocks contrast with and set off plants, stones, and wood so well that we often place them in full view as integral components of the design (see figures 4-10, 7-5, and 8-3). Occasionally we have to customize a pot. When a plant is in a plastic pot that is so deep that it cannot be hidden in the arrangement (assuming the arrangement calls for it to be hidden), we customize it. Warming the pot in hot water softens the plastic and makes it easy to cut off the top with a pair of scissors. In this way we make bulb pans out of standard pots in sizes that are not available commercially. These are particularly useful for Selaginella and other plants used in the foreground, as well as for small succulents for desert scenes

Undoubtedly other people will find all sorts of other materials to use in the infrastructure. It's a catch-as-catch-can game, and we enjoy the sport of it.

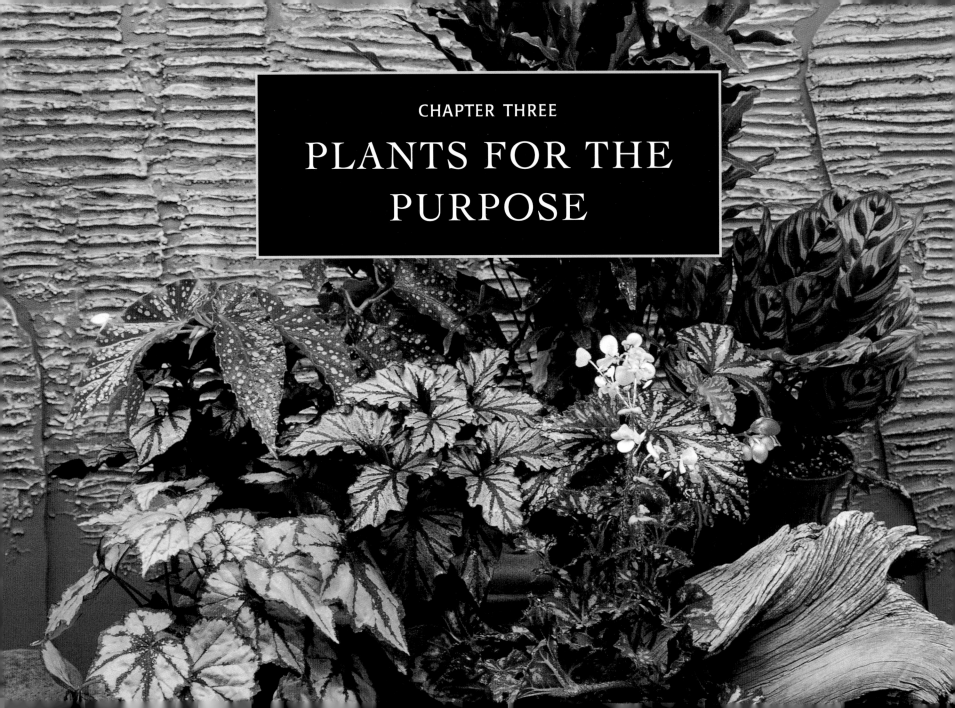

CHAPTER THREE

PLANTS FOR THE PURPOSE

The effectiveness of a landscape should not depend on the specific plants used in the design—we preach this over and over again. But the urge to use plants and more plants can be irresistible. This particularly can be the case with plants that are rare, difficult to cultivate, reluctant to bloom but blooming nevertheless, or so singularly beautiful that they capture our gaze and refuse to let it go. In other words, the plants that we most want to show off are those that require an enormous amount of time and effort to maintain and would rob the design of its unity—they are exactly the kinds of plants you should avoid.

But plants do play a role in most interior landscape design—often an essential role. The plants set off the architectural quality of the piece and emphasize the geometry of the composition and the permanence of the infrastructure. Conversely, the infrastructure forms a stage on which the plants can really shine, not individually but rather as an ensemble. In such a setting, orchids deserve their title "queen of flowers," bromeliads show off their statuesque geometry and intricate patterns, and ferns add their filigree grace. But even the humblest mosses, liverworts, and lichens can play supporting roles as ground covers to extraordinary effect. And all of this is in the service of the entire design, which is our major concern.

What are the best plants to use in furnishing an interior landscape? It depends. Of course, the effect desired is a primary factor. The time, energy, and expense needed to obtain the effect and maintain it are also important. The conditions under which the plants will be grown affect the decision, as do the personal taste of the designer, the intended audience, and the client who is footing the bill.

A designer choosing plants always will have to make compromises: the space allotted for the setting might not measure up to the designer's imagination; the "perfect" plants for the project may be unobtainable; perhaps the lighting is inadequate, the temperature is wrong, or the humidity is too low. Fortunately, there is enough diversity in the plant kingdom to guarantee that a compromise can be found.

What are the best plants for the purpose? Of course, we have our personal favorites and have chosen to use them in many of our designs. But these plants are not the only good choices. They are good, however, in that most of them are well known, widely available, and considered by most to be easy to grow. To be included in our preferred list, a plant had to be more than interesting or merely beautiful. It had to be an easy keeper with a strong constitution and no special needs. Temperature requirements had to be met easily—no arctic mosses were entertained. Light demands had to be moderate or low—we passed over those obligate sun dwellers that elongate at the first shadow and gave the nod to the plants that tolerate shade. (The intensity of indoor lighting is nowhere near that of natural outdoor lighting, making shade lovers particularly appropriate for indoor landscapes.) And humidity demands had to be reasonable—no New Zealand filmy ferns or Dracula orchids from the high Andes. We wanted plants that would perform reliably year-round, ruling out American pitcher plants (too bad, for we love them). Plants had to be disease- and insect-resistant, or at least resistant to reasonably safe fungicides and pesticides—goodbye to most ivies and many gesneriads. The plants had to be fairly slow-growing and not need frequent pinching back or repotting. We love flowers, but not when frequent deadheading is needed; this eliminated the sinningia from consideration and nearly omitted streptocarpus. Phototropism was not viewed as a redeeming feature. The inability to color up under moderate light was a trait that blocked certain bromeliads, crassulas, and other succulents from consideration. And too much beauty, pizzazz, or individuality was enough to bar the showoffs—no coleus, no rex begonias, no standard cattleyas.

The root system of the plant was also a consideration. Too massive a root system—one that required too large a pot—excluded the plant from the list. This eliminated some calatheas and ferns. On the other hand, the big, old, fuzzy feet of ferns like the aglaomorphas (see figures 6-6 and 9-20) and davallias are so striking and unusual that they were included. Some orchids were included partly because of the decorative quality of their wildly wandering roots, unusually thick and covered with a silvery hydroscopic sheath (see figure 4-4).

We do almost no shaping of plants, and we are careful to choose plants that require no shaping. Most herbaceous tropicals strongly resent attempts to alter their natural shape—to reconfigure them is to disfigure them. So except for light pruning and occasional division of overgrown specimens, we leave them alone. We may use a bamboo or wire stake to give temporary support to a flower stem, but we even try to avoid this in the name of low maintenance. Moreover, the support is unlikely to be a design asset.

Here are a few of the plants we consider best for the purpose. We have arranged them into groups of similar plants—similar in landscape effect, similar in requirements, or similar taxonomically. Our list of best performers includes:

Aralias
Arums
Begonias
Brassaias
Bromeliads
Carnivorous plants (of several families)
Cycads
Ferns (of several families)
Figs
Gesneriads
Lilies
Orchids
Palms
Peperomias
Prayer plants
Spikemosses
Succulents (of several families, including cactus)
Primitives
Miscellaneous plants that do not fit into the above categories

We seldom mention the size of a plant—an omission we excuse on several grounds. Growing conditions, pruning methods, the age of the plant, and the clone can greatly affect a plant's size. For example, some tropical pitcher plants (*Nepenthes*) are vines that can scramble up a tree for more then 40 ft (12 m), yet may be grown in a terrarium as a cluster of low rosettes by cramping the roots and repeatedly pruning the tip growth. Properly managed, they will retain their dwarf status for an indefinite period of time.

Plant nomenclature is a confused and confusing topic, and we have tried to follow convention as much as possible. Family names are capitalized and set in roman type, but when used in the vernacular, capitalization is not required. For example, the aralia family is Araliaceae. Almost all family names end in the suffix "aceae." The palm family, Palmae, is one of the few exceptions.

As is customary, we use italics when writing the genus and species of a plant, and we capitalize the first letter of the genus but not of the species: For example, the plant with the common name "whisk fern" has the scientific name "*Psilotum nudum*," "*Psilotum*" being the genus and "*nudum*" the species. The hybrid slipper orchid *Paphiopedilum* Maudiae is a cross between two species, *Paphiopedilum callosum* and *Paphiopedilum lawrenceanum*. Maudiae is not a species but rather the name of this cross, and is not italicized; it is capitalized only because it is derived from a proper noun. *Paphiopedilum* Maudiae 'Magnificum' is a specific clone of that cross.

Vernacular names are set without capitals, except when the name involves a proper noun. This is the case even when the vernacular name and scientific name coincide. For example, begonia is the vernacular of *Begonia*. Because "genus" is singular, any plural form is in the vernacular, so we write "peperomias" and not "Peperomias."

In some cases, we were not able to make a full determination of the plant we used. For example, "*Begonia* hybrid" in the list refers to a plant that we know to be a begonia hybrid, but we don't know which hybrid it happens to be. Similarly, "*Aloe* species" refers to an aloe, but we were not able to determine the species. There is one case where we could not even pin down the genus of the plant with any certainty—*Aglaomorpha* or *Drynaria*—both of these listings refer to the same plant. It is often extremely difficult to determine the species of a plant that is not reproductively mature. And in some cases, even the experts may not agree on a plant's name.

Aralia Family
(Araliaceae)

Ornamental genera for indoors: *Brassaia* (also known as *Shefflera*), *Fatsia*, *Hedera*, *Polyscias*

The aralia family has many popular members. Although some are too big, some are too buggy, and some are just too coarse, a couple are true treasures. Our favorite is *Brassaia arboricola*. It can grow to a bushy 6 ft (1.8 m) and has fans of eight leaflets; each leaflet can be up to 6 in (15 cm) long. But even better is a dwarf clone that grows to half this height, with leaves reduced proportionately. We use this plant and its variegated counterpart repeatedly (see figures 4-12, 6-7, and 9-17). Its growth rate is moderate, its cultural demands are slight (although mealybugs may be a problem), and its light demands are modest. It is readily available and easy to propagate. Top pruning promotes bushiness and controls growth, although the plant is often reluctant to branch. It has an unpretentious elegance that makes it a perfect foil for other plants while maintaining its own character.

The Ming aralia (*Polyscias fruticosa*) is our other favorite in the aralia family. It can grow to a height of 10 ft (3 m) into a naturally picturesque form of a crooked tree with gnarly branches. The leaves are 5 in (12.5 cm) long but crested like parsley, so that each leaf looks like a clump of finer leaves. Squint, and the tree looks like bonsai, justifying the vernacular "Ming aralia." We grow a dwarf clone 'Elegans,' and have used it in several pieces (see figures 6-2 and 8-14). It is a tolerant plant and easy to grow, although it occasionally drops leaves just to aggravate us.

Arum Family
(Araceae)

Ornamental genera for indoors: *Aglaonema, Alocasia, Anthurium, Diffenbachia, Monstera, Philodendron, Spathiphyllum, Syngonium, Zantedeschia*

Some of the dandiest members of the plant kingdom reside here—which isn't to say that this is a particularly garish clan. Most arums have rather modest blossoms and are grown for their leaves. Exceptions include the peace lily (*Spathiphyllum*, see figure 4-9), the calla lily (*Zantedeschia*), and some of the anthuriums (see figure 4-4), but even these won't embarrass you when out of bloom.

Many of the anthuriums have leaves with scalloped margins and the shiny texture of patent leather. In some with near-black leaves, the veins are bold and silvery white. *Alocasia* x amazonica (see figure 4-8) has all of these features. Others are the color of pewter or copper and have marvelously quilted surfaces.

The anthuriums are also notable for the texture, shape, color, and venation of their leaves. *Anthurium clarinervon* and *A. crystallinum* have black-green heart-shaped leaves the texture of velvet, with a vein pattern as striking as that of *Anthurium* x amazonica.

Philodendrons and monsteras are among the most popular indoor plants, renowned for their big, bold leathery leaves in a variety of wonderful shapes—scalloped, digitate, or (as in *Monstera*) perforated. Some philodendrons have burgundy leaves, and some are so yellow they seem to beg for a shot of iron. But most are green, silvery white, or nearly black.

These are wonderful plants, and some have to be ranked among the most beautiful in the world. Most have low to moderate light requirements and adapt well to culture under lights. We would grow and use many more than we do if more were available in smaller sizes. We would love to work with a dwarf *Philodendron selloum*, but we cannot find one. A series of dwarf philodendrons, alocasias, and anthuriums could have some commercial value—but none has been developed. Perhaps the Dutch can do for these plants what they have done for the figs (*Ficus*)—patent and market a series of worthwhile dwarfs.

Most philodendrons and spathiphyllums thrive in the low humidity of homes and offices, but the other genera appreciate more humidity. Light requirements are quite modest for most arums, and they are fairly disease-resistant, although we have had significant problems with spider mites on anthuriums.

Besides the dandies mentioned above, there are three other genera of enormous popularity: *Aglaonema*, *Spathiphyllum*, and *Syngonium*. Although none of these are great beauties, all are durable, inexpensive, and readily available. Their popularity makes them unexciting choices as single specimens on a desktop or floor stand, but for our purposes they do just fine, providing pleasant background greenery that sets off their companions without stealing the show (see figures 4-3, 9-1, and 9-17). Spathiphyllums in flower are attractive but not ostentatious (figure 4-9)—it's too bad that more dwarf forms are not available, as we certainly could use them.

3-1 A few begonias and a couple of calatheas

Begonia Family
(Begoniaceae)

Ornamental genera for indoors: *Begonia*

These are premier plants for our purpose and we use them again and again (see figures 4-7, 6-10, and 8-12, and figure 3-1 for a family portrait). Though some are grown for their flowers, our interest in them rests primarily with their leaves. In some sections of the genus, the rex hybrids in particular, the puckered silken leaves are colored in rose, black, green, and silver, in patterns so ornate as to shame the most lavish brocade. However, there are others that are more modest, and these actually serve us much better.

The rhizomatous, caudiciform, fibrous, and angel-wing begonias offer species and hybrids with smaller leaves and less ostentatious patterns, but they are striking nevertheless. Moreover, they are less finicky in their needs and less fragile in constitution than the rex begonias. Ours have not been bothered by insects or disease. But, as is the case with their royal brothers, the rex begonias, they grow sloppy with age and must be restarted from stem cuttings several times a year—the only major drawback to these otherwise useful plants.

We grow all of our begonias in glass-walled cases with a day temperature of 75° F (23.9° C) and a night temperature of 65° F (18.3° C). Air circulation is good, light is low to moderate from full-spectrum fluorescents, and humidity is approximately 50 percent during the day and 70 percent at night.

As you will see in the examples, we use begonias when we want to mass a color other than green against a group of predominantly green plants. For this we grow several dwarf cultivars with leaves predominantly of silver, of green with silver blotches, or of gold (see figures 4-7, 4-9, and 6-11).

Bromeliad Family
(Bromeliaceae)

Ornamental genera for indoors: *Aechmea, Billbergia, Cryptanthus, Neoregelia, Tillandsia*, and *Vriesea*

This is a large family of plants whose most prominent members might be the pineapple (*Ananas sativus*) and Spanish moss (*Tillandsia usneoides*). But it is the others in the family that attract the plant hobbyists. The addiction to bromeliads is easy to understand, given their willingness to hybridize and their great variety of colors, patterns, and shapes. But generally these plants are the darlings of the outdoor gardeners living in frost-free climates or northern folk who have greenhouses. It is not that indoor gardeners have been left out, it's just that they must be a bit more choosy in their selection.

All of the genera just mentioned, except for the air plants (*Tillandsia*), are tank plants—plants that form water-holding vessels out of more-or-less upright leaves. These vessels range from the elegantly narrow tubes of billbergia to the widespreading star-shaped saucers of cryptanthus. Because of their statuesque quality, their thick but translucent leaves, and their sharply delineated color patterns (spots, blotches, longitudinal stripes, transverse bands, and feathering), tank plants are great show pieces and are best used singly or in small groups as highlights in the landscape.

The color and form of most of the aechmeas, billbergias, and neoregelias depends heavily on the strength, quality, and duration of the light they receive. If the light is inadequate, many will splay sloppily and their color and patterns will fade. Nevertheless, there are several that perform well enough in window light and fluorescent light to be considered for use in interior landscapes (see figure 4-11).

The vrieseas are also tank plants, but most are considerably more tolerant of lower light levels. Many don't show quite the variety of form and color as some of those just mentioned, but *Vriesea simplex* is a showstopper, and *V. fosteriana, V. hieroglyphica*, and *V. fenestralis* are among the most beautiful of all, although they are too large for our applications. Smaller vrieseas are pictured in figures 4-2 and 4-11.

The earth stars (*Cryptanthus*) generally are more splayed, forming loose rosettes with few leaves that hold very little water. Their starlike form and terrestrial habit give them their common name—earth stars. They are as beautifully marked as any bromeliad, and some rank among the world's most beautiful foliage plants (see figure 9-20 for one of our favorites, *C. fosterianus*). They are also less demanding of light.

Aechmeas, billbergias, neoregelias, and vrieseas can be grown as epiphytes, though some require that their roots be wrapped in long-fiber sphagnum moss. In our collection, most are grown in small pots. The tank bromeliads should have water in their centers at all times. Scale insects may be a problem for some, but otherwise they are a good choice: Most are disease- and pest-resistant, quite adaptable, slow-growing, and very easy to care for.

Air plants (*Tillandsia*) are just that—plants that absorb nutrients and moisture from the air; their roots merely anchor them. Pot them in a nice rich soil, and the entire plant is likely to rot away. Glue or wire them to a twig or branch, and they'll be happy and look their best. Most are small and the variety is great: fuzzballs, porcupines, sea urchins, and vriesea impersonators are all represented. Some look like Dr. Seuss characters, others like deranged starfish. Color is limited—mostly gray or silver, some green, and an occasional blush of red. Some are moisture lovers (mesic) and others prefer dryer conditions (xeric); some even live aboard cacti. We love these beautiful, strange plants and we use them to ornament naked branches or twigs (see figures 4-3, 4-7, and 6-10). Most require high light and airy conditions, but placing them high on twigs satisfies these requirements. Most will settle in quite happily if they are sprayed with a very diluted solution of fertil-izer once or twice a week and if the more finicky ones are misted daily.

Although several of our landscapes show a bromeliad or two in bloom, we do not grow them for their inflorescences, as gorgeous, spectacular, and bizarre as they are. True, some remain in flower for months, and some attend their flowering with a special flush of long-lasting leaf color. However, they flower only once on a rosette, and a pup (sideshoot) may take several years to reach flowering size. Moreover, typical interior growing conditions are inadequate for flowering many of the bromeliads. So we grow them for their incomparable foliage, and that is quite enough.

Carnivorous plants
(several families)

Ornamental genera for indoors: *Cephalotus* (Cephalotaceae); *Dionaea*, *Drosera* (Droseraceae); *Nepenthes* (Nepenthaceae); *Pinguicula*, *Utricularia* (Lentibulariaceae); *Sarracenia* (Sarraceniaceae)

What can be more entertaining than a glass case full of ravenous carnivorous plants? Every so often, when the mood strikes you, you throw in a hapless insect and watch it get snapped up by the bear-trap jaws of a Venus's-flytrap (*Dionaea muscipula*), writhe out its time in the sticky clutches of a sundew (*Drosera*), or thrash out its life in the digestive juices of a pitcher plant's pitcher (*Cephalotus*, *Heliamphora*, *Nepenthes*, *Sarracenia*).

But you don't have to be ghoulish to get your jollies out of this collection of plants. They are of such singular beauty that they are worth growing for their appearance alone, never mind their sinister nature. Several of them are pictured in figure 3-2.

Consider the tropical pitcher plants (*Nepenthes*, figure 3-2). Shrubby or, more often, vinelike, some can be grown as short-stature rosettes with a bit of under-potting and pruning. The leaf tips of these wonderfully diabolical works of nature extend into tendril-like structures sometimes more than 1 ft (0.3 m) long, at the end of which dangles an upright pitcher, partly full of insect attractants and digestive juices. These pitchers, up to 14 in (35 cm) long in some species, are true works of art. Their shape can be that of a barrel, gravy boat, wine goblet, tapered vase, or toilet bowl complete with toilet seat and cover. The body of the pitcher can be solidly colored in yellow, pink, red, or green, or it may be spotted, stippled, or streaked with burgundy. The mouth of the pitcher is rimmed with a collar (perianth)—jadelike in texture, wide and flaring or narrow and rolled, nearly smooth or transversely ridged with distinct teeth. This collar can be burgundy in color, lime green, or something in between, with or without transverse banding of a different color. A cap (operculum) opens over the mouth of the pitcher and may be situated above the mouth like an umbrella or even tilted backward like the visor of a baseball cap worn by a kid with attitude. No wonder these plants were loved by the Victorians.

In spite of their distinct character, *Nepenthes* (see figures 3-2, 4-4, 4-9, and 4-14) aren't widely coveted today, perhaps because few people realize that many can be grown with no trouble at all. Many of the hybrids and several of the species tolerate moderate light and moderate humidity, even to the extent that they thrive on an east-facing windowsill.

Another of our favorite genera is *Pinguicula*, the butterworts. These form rosettes of bright green sticky leaves on plants from less than 1 in (2.5 cm) to more than 6 in (15 cm) across, depending on the species. The sticky leaves trap insects—the plant kingdom's flypaper. The flowers range from beautiful to spectacular, and in several species are presented over a period of many months. The butterworts are among our favorite carnivores, and we have used them many times (see figure 4-10). They are easy to care for and are fairly flexible in their temperature, light, and humidity needs.

Nepenthes and *Pinguicula* are the carnivorous genera represented in our arrangements. But there are several others that, in the right location, would be an asset to an interior landscape. The West Australian pitcher plant (*Cephalotus follicularis*) is a miniature only a few inches high and wide with pitchers of the same design as those of nepenthes. Under the right conditions, the 1- to 3-in (2.5- to 7.5-cm) pitchers are deep red. The pitchers encircle a rosette of leaves and rest on the ground. This is an excellent terrarium subject but will languish if the humidity is below 40 percent.

Another genus to consider is *Drosera*, the sundews. These are mostly small plants, from less than an inch across to several inches, with leaves that are narrow and arranged like pins on a pincushion or paddle-

3-2 For the ghoulish at heart, a family portrait of carnivorous plants, with a bit of Spanish moss and a whisk fern, a prefern primitive

shaped and arranged in a rosette. The leaves are covered with slender polyp-like protuberances, each of which ends in a sticky globule that attracts and holds insect prey. In some species a red color suffuses the entire leaf and the glasslike globules, giving the entire plant the look of a gem-encrusted brooch. Many of the sundews are seasonal, but some from the tropics and subtropics thrive year-round under warm terrarium conditions.

Still another genus of perfect candidates for a terrarium featuring carnivorous plants is *Utricularia*, the bladderwort genus—what an unlovely name for a genus that has so many wonderful plants. These are carnivorous by reason of their nearly microscopic, spring-loaded, flask-shaped traps on the roots. Opening on contact, the trap sucks in microscopic prey. Some of the bladderworts are aquatic, some are epiphytic, and some are terrestrial. It's the latter that we have in mind—plants like *Utricularia saundersii*, mat-forming with 0.25-in (0.6-cm) leaves and 2-in (5-cm) tall racemes of relatively large white flowers. In bloom,

this plant resembles a miniature stand of foxgloves, except that each flower looks like the head of a white rabbit. It flowers for months, but it's a charmer in bloom or not.

Some of the most beautiful and wondrous carnivores are not on our list because of one damnable fault—they require months of dormancy in a cold lockup. The Venus's-flytrap (*Dionaea muscipula*), the cobra pitcher (*Darlingtonia californica*), and the half-dozen American pitcher plants (*Sarracenia*) and their hybrids were omitted for this reason. Too bad, because they are beautiful, fascinating plants. However, we do grow a few, and you can see one in figure 3-2.

Cycad Families
(Cycadaceae and Zamiaceae)

Ornamental genera for indoors: *Cycas, Dioon, Encephalartos, Zamia*

The cycads are primitive plants that evolved more than two million years ago, and they are built to last. Squat, heavy trunks are the norm and they often look like monstrous pineapples. Leaves are palmlike, but often enormously thick and sometimes armed like a vicious holly.

Most are desert plants but some tolerate a bit of shade and humidity. Many are too tall or too wide for our purposes, and many are too odd to play an ensemble role. Cycads grow so slowly that well-grown plants of good size are worth a ransom. In fact, cycad-nabbing from gardens was a criminal enterprise in California in the 1960s: From moving pickup trucks, bandits lassoed them, yanked them out of the ground, and sped off with them.

We love these strange plants, but space limitations prevent us from growing more than three: *Cycas revoluta, Zamia floridana*, and *Zamia furfuracea*. The sago palm (*C. revoluta*) can grow as tall as 10 ft (3 m), but under-potting and an occasional root pruning will keep it to less than 1.5 ft (0.45 m). The plant is almost comical in appearance—a dumpy palm tree—and this makes it difficult to place in an arrangement. However, group three of them in a shallow pot and you already have an arrangement. They probably are best suited for desert setups. In contrast, coontie (*Z. floridana*) (figure 9-17) looks like a graceful fern, if you

ignore its short trunk. *Z. furfuracea*, the third member of our strange triumvirate, is shorter and more wide-spreading than the other two. The leaves, bipinnate like the others, can reach a length of 3 ft (0.9 m), but again under-potting will check the growth to less than 1 ft (0.3 m). The leaflets, broadly elliptical to 2 in (5 cm), are as thick as cardboard.

Ferns
(several families)

Ornamental genera for indoors: *Adiantum, Aglaomorpha, Hemionitis, Pellaea, Pteris, Vittaria* (Adiantaceae); *Asplenium, Dryopteris* (Aspleniaceae); *Blechnum, Doodia* (Blechnaceae); *Davallia, Humata, Nephrolepis* (Davalliaceae); *Trichomanes* (Hymenophyllaceae); *Drynaria, Microsorum, Platycerium, Polypodium, Pyrrosia* (Polypodiaceae)

Ferns and their allies (horsetails, mosses, liverworts, and others) are among the most ancient plants, tracing their lineage back some 400 million years. Once they dominated the planet, and even today there are about 8,500 species. They grow on every continent in almost every ecological niche, from the tropics to the arctic regions, from water habitats to the deserts. So it is not surprising that many of the plants are ideal choices for the indoor garden. We will mention only a few that we have used most frequently.

Diversity of form among the ferns is so great that every effect from bold to delicate can be achieved using them. For a delicate, airy effect, there are no better candidates than the maidenhair ferns (*Adiantum*), the rabbit's-foot and hare's-foot ferns (*Davallia, Humata*), and some of the sword ferns (*Nephrolepis*) (see figures 4-1, 4-2, and 4-4). Somewhat bolder (or coarser, if it's slander you prefer) in texture are the aglaomorphas and drynarias. These and the davallias and humatas have furry roots—a tangle of pipe cleaners, big rabbit feet, or even bigger bear paws, depending on the species—which can be as amusing as they are ornamental (see figures 4-1, 6-6, and 9-20).

Bolder still are *Asplenium, Microsorum,* and *Pyrrosia*. The ferns in the first two genera grow well and are displayed well in pots; those in the

third seem better adapted to life on a mount, and that is the way we like to see them displayed. All have undivided fronds, bright green in the first two, matte green with felted gray-green undersides in the third.

The bird's nest fern (*Asplenium nidus*) is represented here by the cultivar 'Curly' (see figures 4-15 and 9-15). We do not know the ultimate size of the fern but it is slow-growing enough to avoid any problems of size for a long time. Another thoroughly delightful cultivar is the 'Lasagna Fern,' with fronds rippled like its namesake noodle. We grew one to nearly 30 in (75 cm) before reluctantly getting rid of it. It's a conversation piece. These aspleniums form rosettes and do not multiply readily by offsets, although tissue culture of the cultivars supplies the trade.

Microsorum (also known as *Polypodium*) is represented here by *M. punctatum* 'Grandiceps' and *P. c.* 'Cristatum Dwarf' (see figures 6-7 and 6-13). Both grow to about 14 in (35 cm) and the difference between them is very subtle. Most microsorums have simple, straplike fronds

of a very bright green color. But these cultivars have widely forked and crestate fronds. Growth is fairly upright and compact, but somewhat disorganized. Plants are easily divided.

Recently we have obtained a much smaller (10-in, or 25-cm), more congested crestate microsorum that is even easier to grow and propagate (see figure 4-12); we love it, but we don't know the species or the cultivar. Maybe it will grow up to be one of the above.

The Japanese felt fern (*Pyrrosia lingua*) has strap-shaped fronds in the wild form and all sorts of crestate cultivars. Our favorite is 'Obaki' (Japanese for "monster"), which has felted fronds to about 7 in (17.5 cm) (see figures 6-7 and 6-9). This, too, is an easy grower, increasing slowly but steadily and rambling over its mount according to its own roadmap—a superb fern in spite of its disorganized growth habit.

Bolder by far are the staghorn ferns (*Platycerium*), epiphytic ferns with antlerlike fertile fronds and shieldlike sterile fronds that plaster themselves against the support. The

larger species, like *P. grande*, can span 8 ft (2.5 m) from top to bottom, although young specimens remain small enough for indoor display for many years (see figure 6-10). The elephant ear (or cabbage) staghorn (*P. elephantotis*) can reach over 4 ft (1.2 m), and it too is slow-growing enough to remain in bounds for many years (see figures 6-4 and 6-6). Smaller species such as *P. ellisii* (see figure 4-1) and smaller cultivars such as *P. bifurcatum* 'Dwarf' (see figure 4-1) span 14 to 18 in (35 to 45 cm) when fully mature and are useful at every stage of growth. These magnificent ferns are showpieces in any setting—bold enough to maintain their individuality, yet easily assimilated into an arrangement.

Several other ferns are bit players in our arrangements, but those already mentioned have become our regulars—they are beautiful, easy to grow, and easy to manage. Few plants are as useful.

Fig Family
(Moraceae)

Ornamental genus for indoors: *Ficus*

The weeping fig (*Ficus benjamina*) may be the most popular indoor tree in the 4- to 7-ft (1.2- to 2-m) range. It's a tolerant tree, growing in fairly low to fairly high light, cool-house to hothouse temperatures, and living-room to hothouse humidity. All sorts of cultivars are available: Forms have been selected for their variegated leaves, twisted leaves, dwarf stature, and clumping habit. Many of these were developed in Holland and are patented. There are several that we like, including the old-fashioned unadorned original. It's a superb background plant, is well adapted to indoor growing, and immediately establishes the mood of a tropical forest.

But we also use *Ficus fakius*, a fake fig made of cloth, wire, dead wood, and plastic (figures 6-2, 6-9, and 6-12). *Ficus fakius* is even more tolerant than *F. benjamina* and can be stored like cordwood and totally ignored until needed. Moreover, it can be mercilessly pruned and twisted into shape. Even the prunings can be used, and you can be confident that they will retain their fresh green appearance for a long, long time.

The only other figs we use are *Ficus pumila* cultivars. Pumila means "small," and small these plants are, with leaves 0.5 in (1.2 cm) or less on slender vining stems. They are undemanding in their light requirements but need a fair amount of humidity (40 percent or better) and constant moisture at the roots. Our favorite cultivars are the oak leaf miniature fig (*F. p.* 'Quercifolia') and the variegated miniature fig (*F. p.* 'Variegata'). The first has puckered leaves shaped like those of a white oak but only 0.25 in (0.6 cm) across (see figure 9-13); the second has leaves that are 0.5 in (1.2 cm) across and heavily margined in white (see figures 4-14, 6-3, and 9-1). These are very useful plants for draping over stone or wood to soften hard edges in the landscape.

Care could not be simpler. House plant mix (2 parts sphagnum peat moss, 1 part perlite, 1 part vermiculite) is good enough. The light equivalent of an east window exposure is adequate. Water demands are moderate. Although the tree forms are quite resistant to bugs and diseases, the miniature creepers are less so and need more humidity.

There are many other species and cultivars of *Ficus* that have been proven useful under the conditions we require. Only space constraints have kept our collection to those that we have described. But keep in mind the potential of this genus of excellent plants.

Gesneriad Family
(Gesneriaceae)

Ornamental genera for indoors: *Aeschynanthus, Codonanthe, Columnea, Episcia, Nematanthus, Saintpaulia, Sinningia, Streptocarpus*

These are the darlings of a worldwide fraternity of devotees. The African violet (*Saintpaulia* species) and Gloxinia (*Sinningia* species) are included here, the first promoted by hoards of fans. These plants are popular because of their ease of culture (that of some, at least); their beauty; their enormous variety of forms and sizes; their leaf shapes, textures, colors, and patterns; and their flowers, which also come in a kaleidoscope of patterns, colors, and shapes. Add to this extraordinarily rich gene pool a tendency to mutate and a willingness to hybridize—and what's not to like?

However, many of the plants are irredeemably sloppy. Take streptocarpus, for example. Even the dwarfs look sloppy at maturity, and maturity is reached fairly quickly. Then the strap-shaped leaves outgrow their turgor and sprightly carriage; they droop too easily and the entire plant looks sad and shabby. But we have used them on occasion (see figure 4-4). African violets (*Saintpaulia*) remain neater longer and there are some true minis. They flower frequently and profusely, which necessitates some deadheading chores, but the flowers are undeniably charming. In fact, that is their main problem—they are too cute. They look curiously Victorian—out of place and out of date—not at all at ease in a naturalistic setting and out of character in an abstract setting. In some cases, however, they work just fine (see figure 4-3).

Bugginess is another problem with gesneriads. Mealybugs, which appear as bits of cottony fluff on leaves, stems, and roots, where they sap the plant's juices and usually leave a shiny, sticky residue, love gesneriads. They disfigure leaves, stunt growth, and even can cause the death of the plant. *Streptocarpus*, *Nematanthus*, *Episcia*, and *Codonanthe* are among the most vulnerable genera. We have given up on most of these, but you will notice that we have used a dwarf codonanthe several times (see figures 6-3, 6-11, and 9-20), even while battling the bugs with insecticides.

Lily Family
(Liliaceae)

Ornamental genera for indoors: *Asparagus*, *Chlorophytum*

The asparagus ferns are ferny nonferns in the same genus as the vegetable asparagus. There are several ornamental species, but our favorite is *Asparagus setaceus* in its compact varieties. The standard form looks a lot like the edible species when left uncut and gone to seed. But if the ornamental is left unpruned, it becomes a tangled mess of disheveled plumes on stems that seem to want to climb in order to get

away from themselves. However, with a bit of pruning, the compact selections take on the appearance of a cypress grove, and that is how we love to see them (see figures 5-23 and 9-10). *A. setaceus* is an easy plant to maintain, accepting a wide range of light and temperature conditions and even some dryness in the air and at the roots.

The airplane plants (*Chlorophytum*) include those all-too-common hanging basket types with variegated leaves and long, dangling runners that bear clusters of white flowers and occasionally new plants. These airborne plants can continue to grow until they, too, produce runners with flowers and new plants—the whole mass is dense and a bit disorganized but attractive nevertheless. We use a relatively refined and restrained cultivar, *C. comosum* 'Mandaianum' (see figures 4-12 and 9-1). Its effect is delicate and graceful, provided it doesn't become overgrown. The other chlorophytum that we grow is *C. bichetii*, even more dwarf at 6 in (15 cm). This one prefers to cluster and seldom produces lengthy runners (see figure 4-14). It is almost

grasslike in its effect, making it humbly attractive.

Both of these plants are nearly indestructible, with a wide latitude of acceptable light levels, temperatures, and humidity. They tell you when they are overly dry by drooping. We have had problems with mealybug infestations on *C. bichetii*, but otherwise they have been trouble-free.

Orchid Family
(Orchidaceae)

Ornamental genera for indoors: *Aerangis, Aeranthes, Angraecum, Brassavola, Cattleya, Dendrobium, Haemaria, Masdevallia, Miltonia, Odontoglossum, Oncidium, Paphiopedilum, Phalaenopsis*, and several hybrid genera involving these and others

In our minds, these are the premier flowering plants for our purpose—maybe for any purpose. Orchidaceae is the royal family of the plant kingdom. And what an extended family it is, with about 800 genera and nearly 20,000 species in the wild, from a wide diversity of habitats. Add to that some 50,000 species contrived by humans, in-

cluding fertile hybrids involving eight genera! No wonder so many orchids have found their way into our homes and hearts.

Formerly the playthings of the very wealthy, orchids are now within the budget of most people. You can find live orchid plants for sale in supermarkets and hardware stores—some of these plants are actually suitable for home growing. Many of these orchids grow easily beside African violets, but that juxtaposition is likely to render the latter invisible.

The accessibility of the orchid hobby was brought about by tissue culture techniques that allowed the most coveted orchids (with a few exceptions) to be mass-produced in virtually unlimited numbers. Modern horticultural methods and the development of suitable artificial lighting were also factors. And at least as important was the realization that many of the showiest species were perfectly well adapted to growing in the home. However, it still takes several years to raise an orchid to flowering size, and in most climates they cannot be field grown.

So it is unlikely that they will ever be cheap or common enough to blunt their exotic allure.

It is not merely orchids' former exclusivity that makes them so desirable. The range of flower shapes from bizarre to beautiful, the range of colors from subtle to garish, and the range of markings from controlled to extravagant all play a role. Additionally, some have delicious, exotic fragrances, some offer beautiful and unusual plant forms, and some have highly ornamental leaves.

Orchids can be grown at home at the window or in the basement under lights; greenhouse conditions aren't necessary. All the orchids we grow are among our favorites, but we mention only a few here and certainly do not exhaust the list of those suitable for interior landscapes. Some orchids are better suited to our present purposes than others, and these deserve special mention. Slipper orchids (*Paphiopedilum*) and moth orchids (*Phalaenopsis*) are good plants for beginners because they offer ease of cultivation and bloom reliably over a very

long season. The "paphs," as slipper orchids are nicknamed, are characterized by a pouch-shaped lip. They are among the most beautiful, interesting, and rewarding of all plants to grow. There are too many notable ones to describe, but you will see some of our favorites illustrated in figures 4-1, 4-3, 4-7, 6-12, and in a group portrait in figure 3-3. It is not unusual for individual paph flowers to last for six months. Some paphs, like the Maudiae-type hybrids, flower two and even three times a year. And some of the sequential bloomers, producing successive stems and flower after flower on the same stem, can remain in bloom for years. Nearly all paphs have presentable leaves and plant shapes; some are truly gorgeous and have to be considered among the loveliest of foliage plants. Moreover, they are undemanding regarding light and humidity (as orchids go), which increases their usefulness.

Two faults can be leveled against the paphs. None of the slipper orchids have been cloned, and because it takes years (ten years for some) to grow one from a seed or a

pup to flowering size, and because variability in the hybrids is often great, these orchids remain quite pricey. The second shortcoming of the slipper orchids is their intolerance to stale potting materials; they must be, or at least should be, repotted annually—a small inconvenience given the pleasure they bring.

The second great genus for home growing is *Phalaenopsis*, or "phals," as its members are called. Being amenable to cloning and even less picky about growing conditions than the paphs makes these orchids the ones most frequently offered in supermarkets, hardware stores, and department stores. They, too, are fairly tolerant of low light and low humidity. And their flower display is unexcelled. They can offer twenty magnificent blossoms (to 5 in, or 12.5 cm, across) superbly presented on a long stem (to 4 ft, or 1.2 m). The great variety available—white, pink, white with red lip, yellow, near red, or with patterns in spots, blotches, or stripes—makes these the most popular of all orchids. In fact, for our purposes, they are too gorgeous! They are irrepressible

scene-stealers, and when in flower they take center stage to the exclusion of all else. Nevertheless, we have used some of our more modest phals on occasion (see figure 4-9).

Dendrobium is another highly popular genus often found in supermarkets, hardware stores, and other places that sell fine orchids. Easy to clone, faster to bring to market than paphs and phals, and available in all colors except true blue, these orchids are usually less expensive. There are many different types preferring a wide range of temperatures from cool to intermediate to warm. Most of those in our collection are dwarfs (see figures 4-11, 6-3, and 6-10). They are easy to grow under intermediate to warm conditions and are not as light hungry as other dendrobiums. They bloom for months at a time, often several times a year.

Of the many other excellent choices among the orchids, we'll mention only a few. *Haemaria discolor*, one of several species aptly called "jewel orchids," is a velvety black-leafed beauty whose leaves are lined with a coppery venation. Superb enough even without flowers, it blooms freely with 12-in (30-cm) spikes of small white flowers (see figure 6-7). Such a jewel should be rare and expensive, but in fact it is ridiculously easy to propagate: Just cut off the apical portion of the thick stem with a few leaves attached, dip the cut end into a rooting hormone with fungicide, and pot it. Almost any potting medium will do, even plain water. What is left in the original pot after the harvest will sprout anew, more densely and with greater vigor than before. It's that easy.

Brassavola nodosa is called "lady of the night," and an elegant lady she is, with graceful, off-white, intensely night-fragrant blossoms borne several to a stem (see figure 4-3). Flowers are long-lasting and are produced several times a year. Even the foliage is interesting: stiff narrow leaves of nearly circular cross-section.

The angraecoid orchids (subtribe Angraecinae) include several fabulous genera: *Aerangis, Aeranthes,* and *Angraecum* are the most notable. The flower color is mostly limited to white, but the shapes are wondrous-

3-3 Tropical slipper orchids and an odontocidium

ly distinctive and the flowers are often adorned with long spurs (nectar tubes). The marvelous "king of the angraecums" (*Angraecum sequipedala*) has star-shaped flowers up to 7 in (17.5 cm) across, presented double-file with fourteen to eighteen flowers on a 3-ft (0.9-m) stem. Each blossom sports a 12-in (30-cm) spur below the lip. Upon seeing this extraordinary bloom in Madagascar, Darwin conjectured that it was fertilized by a moth with a 12-in (30-cm) proboscis. The moth was found several years later and named *Xanthopan morgani predicta* to commemorate Darwin's prediction.

The king is too big for our growing space, but we have a wonderful smaller approximation in *Angraecum* Longiscott (see figure 8-15). The flowers are similar but smaller and lightly night-fragrant. But the spur is as long as that of the king. Longiscott inverts its flowers so that the lip is on top. This easy-growing, shade-tolerant hybrid flowers only once a year, but the blossoms last up to two months. Its flowering is an event that we look forward to every year, although the plant itself is distinctively attractive even out of flower.

Angraecum didieri is a miniature gem with relatively large, intensely night-fragrant flowers presented with the lip on the bottom, as is more usual in this genus. The nectar tube is about four times as long as the width of the flower. This little wonder blooms several times a year. The widely rambling thick, white roots are themselves highly ornamental and reason enough to incorporate the plant into a design (see figure 4-4). Adding to its usefulness is its shade tolerance.

Angranthes Grandalena is another of our favorite angraecoids. Its flowers, like a larger version of those of *Angraecum didieri*, grace the plant several times a year (see figure 4-4). This is the most highly awarded intergeneric angraecoid hybrid of all. And it, too, is remarkably shade-tolerant.

The subtribe Oncidiinae is a vast gathering of plants including its flagship genera *Oncidium*, as well as *Miltonia* and *Odontoglossum*. The oncidiums are known as "dancing girl orchids"—see the dorsal sepal as the head of the dancer, the petals as the arms, and the flaring lip as the skirt. The color is usually yellow, often with brown markings, but there are some outstanding exceptions. Flower stems are often branching and carry many flowers. The miltonias are the "pansy orchids," with pansy-shaped and pansy-patterned flowers. The odontoglossums, or "odonts," bear many stunning, often agate-patterned blossoms on a long stem. The pansy orchids and the odonts are usually cool-growing. Many of the oncidiums are intermediate- to warm-growing. Odontocidiums (hybrids between odontoglossums and oncidiums) and miltonidiums (hybrids between miltonias and oncidiums) often show considerable hybrid vigor: increased temperature tolerance, increased acceptance of lower light levels, and a tendency to flower more than once a year.

Miltonidium Pupukea 'Sunset' (see figure 8-2) enjoys all of these benefits in spite of its hideous name. But perhaps the name Pupukea is justified by the plant's scent. One of our absolute favorites is *Miltonidium* Cleo's Pride (see figures 6-4 and 6-10), which bears many-flowered racemes of small (1-in, or 2.5-cm) pale green flowers marked with burgundy blotches. With these recent successes to fuel the imagination, we look forward to many more superb hybrids to follow these lines of breeding.

When orchids are mentioned, most people think of the cattleyas and their hybrids (with other members of the tribe Epidendreae). These big, blowsy orchids used to be the standard for those going to the prom. In fact, they are better suited to the bodice of the belle of the ball than they are to a landscape. They are much too ostentatious to be easy mixers. We do grow a few miniatures modest enough to play a supporting role, but we did not use them in this series of landscapes because even the small ones are a bit too showy. Also, in order to bloom most require more light than is achievable in an interior landscape. And most of the miniatures, especially those with red or pink flowers (from *Sophronites* parents), need a nighttime temperature drop much greater than that a building could provide.

Although you won't see any of them in the landscapes featured here, we have to mention the subtribe Pleurothallidinae, a collection of gorgeous weirdos and grotesqueries that only a sideshow huckster could properly promote. Their main fault, and it's a serious one, is their need for high humidity. But what fascination they would add to a terrarium landscape of modest size!

Dracula is one of the pleurothallid genera, and *vampira* is one of its species. How far can the orchidists go with it? Shamelessly, they have named a clone 'Nosferatu,' after the classic 1922 vampire film. With all its blackness, hair, and pimples it does have a fiendish appearance, and only its cuteness and the fact that it's just an orchid prevent it from being really scary. Here we will give no further account of the no-account count's namesake, as it prefers cryptlike temperatures. In fact, many of the pleurothallids require dripping high humidity and cool temperatures.

In *Masdavallia* (the most popular genus among the pleurothallids), there are many species that thrive under intermediate temperatures. One of our favorites is *M. triangularis*—each apex of their nearly everblooming flat, triangular flowers extends into a long tail. *M. schlimii* is another long-flowering easy grower with yellow-tailed burgundy flowers. Angel Frost is our favorite hybrid; orange-flowered with purple hairs, it blooms from winter through spring, with an occasional blossom now and then throughout the rest of the year. We grow these masdavallias and more but use them only in high-humidity setups.

Ristrepia is another fabulous genus among the pleurothallids. We grow a couple of species; *R. striata* is our favorite. Actually, we are not certain of the name—so many are similar, and the taxonomists continue to wage their name-calling wars over this genus. The flowers are buglike with stringlike petals for antennae and a red-striped yellow lip for carapace and abdomen. Flowers are born only one to a stem and last only a few days. But many stems arise from the back of each leaf and flowering occurs throughout the year. This plant also needs a high-humidity setup.

Palm Family
(Palmae)

Ornamental genera for indoors: *Caryota, Chamaedorea, Chamaerops, Chrysalidocarpus, Licuala, Phoenix, Reinhartia, Rhapis*

Palms have been popular as indoor decorations for centuries. Elegant and stately, they were considered the perfect plants for a sitting room or parlor. Today, palms may seem a bit clichéd, old-fashioned, or too Victorian. At least this is true of the most common parlor palm, *Chrysalidocarpus lutecens*, called the "butterfly palm" or "areca palm" in the nursery trade.

For our purposes, the butterfly palm is best grown under-potted as a congested clump of juveniles about 18 in (45 cm) tall. But they can be irredeemably buggy (mealybugs in particular adore them), and we finally abandoned all that we grew.

Although palms are magnificent plants, many require greenhouse conditions of warmth, light, and humidity in order to thrive. Others are just too big for our limited growing space. However, there are certainly some palms worth considering for use in interior landscapes. The bamboo palms (*Chamaedorea*) and the lady palms (*Rhapis*) are two prime candidates. The first are tall, elegant, clump-forming palms such as *C. erumpens*, to 10 ft (3 m), and *C. seifrizii*, to 6 ft (1.8 m). The stems appear jointed like the culms of bamboo, and the foliage is reminiscent of the fronds of a bipinnate fern. The lady palms are simply magnificent. *R. excelsea* is the lady palm of first choice, and there are cultivars from 1.5 ft (0.45 m) to 15 ft (4.5 m). Some varieties have broad leaves; others have narrow leaves. The leaf color is deep green, but there are yellow forms and a wide variety of variegated forms. The lady palm's growth is excruciatingly slow, and the variegated forms are (supposedly) unstable under micropropagation. This makes the plants quite expensive. According to Mabberly (see the bibliography), the culture of the variegated forms is a cult practice in Japan on a par with tulipmania and is undertaken as a hedge against inflation. By growing and dividing their plants, the owners multiply their fortunes.

Both the bamboo palms and the lady palms are easy to grow even under moderate light. For the purpose of interior landscape design, the lady palm and *Brassaia arboricola* have a similar effect. Because the latter is inexpensive, readily obtainable, easy to propagate, and grows more quickly, we usually ignore the more aristocratic lady. (In horticulture this is called "the bitter grape strategy.") However, we can think of no substitute for the bamboo palms and hence no excuse for not growing them and using them.

Peperomia Family

(Peperomiacea or Piperaceae)

Ornamental genus for indoors: *Peperomia*

Perhaps the most common are too common to notice, but in the vast genus *Peperomia* there are many superb plants that are useful for our purpose. *Peps* is the title of the official *Peperomia* newsletter, and "peps" is what aficionados call the plants.

Peperomia caperata 'Emerald Ripple' (see figure 4-3) is a refined cultivar with shorter and smaller leaves than the species. It has the same deep green color and the same deeply puckered leaves. *P. griseoargentia* is about the size of *P. caperata*, again with deeply puckered leaves but this time the color of pewter. Both make excellent high ground covers. Both are highly shade-tolerant, easy to propagate, and easy to grow—too easy to grow, in fact, for they quickly abandon their youthful comeliness to become overly tall,

loose, and hence sloppy, at which point they have to be restarted (from leaf cuttings in water). But we like them nevertheless.

There are many other peperomias currently in the trade—some shrublets, some vines, even some succulents. There is room in this genus for a great deal of experimentation. No doubt there are many more peps that are shade-tolerant, good-looking, and have restrained growth—peps that are perfect for the purpose of interior landscape design.

Prayer Plant Family

(Marantaceae)

Ornamental genera for indoors: *Calathea, Maranta*

Certainly prayer plants would get their share of votes as the most beautiful foliage plants in the world. They may not exhibit the variety of leaf shapes that the arums have, or the colors of the begonias, but many have a translucence and intricate pattern that has been likened to stained glass. Even those with opaque leaves often have wonderful

designs embossed on their surface. And many have leaves with different colors on each side.

We have tried many prayer plants but have settled for two: the famed peacock prayer plant (*Calathea makoyana*) and *C. rubriginosa*. Figure 3-1 pictures both, and the former also can be seen in many of our landscape pieces in part II. Our peacock prayer plant is an unusual clone, small (to 10 in, or 40 cm) and congested; it grows very slowly. Our *C. rubriginosa* is a tall and stately 20-in (50 cm) plant, with leaves narrower than others that we have seen labeled as the same species. Both are magnificent.

In addition to these two, an almighty congregation of superb prayer plants can be found in local nurseries or ordered from many mail-order nurseries. Some are perfectly suited for use in interior landscapes, but others are a bit too finicky, especially in their need for high humidity, or just too large to fit into many plant collections. Most prayer plants are content under low-light conditions—a definite advantage for use in interior land-

scapes. Their soil requirements are not unusual—a mixture of 2 parts sphagnum peat moss, 1 part perlite, and 1 part vermiculite serves them quite well, although we like to add 2 parts medium-grade fir bark for added drainage. Watering the plants once a week is enough if they are kept in conditions similar to those provided by the glass cases we use, which sustain a day temperature of 75° F (23.9° C), a night temperature of 65° F (18.3° C), a day humidity of 50 percent, a night humidity of 70 percent, and low to moderate light from full-spectrum fluorescents.

What do prayer plants pray for? Deliverance from the scourge of mites, no doubt! Fortunately, most of the prayer plants are tolerant of miticides that hold the mites in check. But keeping up with this problem, as well as the scarcity of small species, has kept us from acquiring a major collection of these plants. The plants' prayer habits are seen by some as another fault: Their appearance changes rather dramatically when they go into their prayer mode, angling their leaves upward and folding them lengthwise. This change occurs in the evening and is more or less independent of the amount of light.

Spikemoss Family
(Selaginellaceae)

Ornamental genus for indoors: *Selaginella*

For a tropical setting, the selaginellas are our favorite ground covers. We find ourselves using them whenever we can—and when we can't, we fake it. For example, figures 6-3 and 9-2 illustrate setups that use real spikemosses where they can grow and fake ones where they can't grow or don't grow as well. (See page 21 for instructions on making fake spikemoss.) Some spikemosses are easier to grow than others, some are too rampant to bother with, some are too tall for our needs, and some are just not as interesting as others.

Selaginella kraussiana and *S. k.* 'Aurea' are two of the best. The first is emerald green; the second is yellow-green (see figure 4-9). Both grow rather too quickly, mounding to 2 in (5 cm) tall and an indeterminate width—soft bright carpets for fairly shaded positions. These spikemosses are quite happy with 40 percent humidity. Much more humidity than that may encourage a looser, less attractive habit. When no-nonsense plants are needed for a bright mossy look, this pair is hard to beat.

But we recently acquired an unnamed (at least its name is unknown to us) selaginella from the Denver Botanic Gardens that we like even more. When mature, this gem stands about 3 in (7.5 cm) tall, layering itself with horizontal sprays of foliage so that a clump takes on the appearance of a dense cypress forest seen from above. The color is more somber than the previous two, but beautiful nevertheless (see figures 4-14 and 6-6). The trick to keeping it neat and tight is to grow it in a shallow container—bulb pans work well. Deeper pots, even azalea pots, cause the plants to grow taller, open up, and slouch sloppily around the pot. Otherwise, growing this gem presents no problems—low to moderate light, humidity around 40 percent or more, and room temperatures suit it perfectly.

Selaginella pallescens is wonderful for its structure, much like the previous selaginella, but taller (to about 8 in, or 20 cm) and more open. However, unless grown under ideal conditions, its beauty soon vanishes, and it becomes rank, sloppy, and floppy. For us, it either grows neatly at an agonizingly slow pace or rushes headlong into dishevelment.

We grow many other selaginellas but haven't yet used them in interior landscapes. Some selaginellas are red and some are a deep shimmering peacock blue, such as the famed *S. uncinata* and *S. wildenovii*. Indeed, the second is called the "peacock selaginella." These plants are scramblers and ramblers, and without control they soon take on an unkempt appearance. The first keeps its meandering to within a few inches of the ground. But the second attempts to lift itself by means of a weak stem and stilt roots to nearly 30 in (75 cm). Shade seems important for the best color, and when mature, few plants are as startlingly beautiful as these are. We grow both of them, but they require much more humidity than is available in an open interior landscape. However, for a large terrarium, they might be perfect.

Perhaps the best-known spikemoss is *Selaginella lepidophylla*, the resurrection fern. This desert dweller curls itself into a ball during the winter months—dry, brown, and seemingly lifeless. But with the rain and warmth of spring, it colors and unfurls into luxuriant ferniness up to a foot tall. The dormant plants are collected and sold in supermarkets and novelty shops to buyers who are instructed to place them in bowls of water to initiate the resurrection. But under these conditions, the renewed life is short-lived, and the plant soon goes down to everlasting dormancy. We have read that a yearly rest period must be respected with this plant, but we know of magnificent specimens growing in cool greenhouses for years without a rest.

Succulents (many families)
Ornamental genera (and their families) for use indoors: *Agave*, *Yucca*

(Agavaceae); *Adenium, Pachypodium* (Apogynaceae); *Ceropegia, Stapelia* (Asclepiadaceae); *Senecio* (Compositae); *Crassula, Echeveria, Sedum, Tacitus, Tylecodon* (Crassulaceae); *Euphorbia, Monadium* (Euphorbiaceae); *Pelargonium, Sarcocaulon* (Geramaceae); *Aloe, Gasteria, Haworthia* (Liliaceae); *Myrmecodia* (Rubia-ceae); and a wide assortment of cacti (Cactaceae)

These are the odd ones. They are chubby, cute, and amusing; stocky, thorny, and menacing; lean, mean, and spiny; and curiously beautiful sculpturally. They are succulents— a term of no taxonomic validity whatsoever that encompasses a vast group of enormously diverse plants from widely separate families. What is their common bond? They are in part quite plump—plump leaves, bloated stems, grossly swollen trunks (caudexes) or aboveground roots, or mixtures of these peculiarities. You find succulents among the geraniums, among the begonias, and of course among the cacti, euphorbias, crassulas, and many more families.

Succulents are eminently collectible: Many are easily cultivated, they are widely diverse in form, and many are interesting and beautiful—all of which makes them difficult to deal with in interior landscape design. With such a vast store of irresistible goodies screaming for your attention, you have to show remarkable restraint. Let down your guard, and you will create an assemblage rather than a coherent design—a hodgepodge collection rather than a landscape in which the parts are subservient to the overall effect. When designing a landscape with succulents, we often turn our backs on some of our favorites. Many are too outrageously gorgeous, too singularly interesting, or simply too different.

Even the more modest ones with quiet good looks sometimes lose control and burst forth with the most extravagant display of outlandish blossoms. This usurps the scene entirely, and the eye focuses on nothing else. But one can not deny them. And when they strut their stuff, we are the first to notice

and applaud. After a few weeks, however, we are ready to see their blossoms fade, and we look forward to watching the design regain its integrity.

With so many diverse families contributing to our list of succulents, it is unreasonable to expect that a single method of cultivation will suit all equally well. Some require nearly full sun exposure; some require a lengthy annual leafless dormancy with no watering; some behave more like annuals rather than perennials. But fortunately many are flexible in their requirements and are well suited for growing indoors. In fact, many are found in the wild growing between rocks or in the company of taller plants and will burn in full sun. The lovers of partial shade often thrive under artificial lights and some will tolerate considerable humidity. We propagate many of our succulents from cuttings placed in glass cases among our orchids.

With so many fascinating and beautiful succulents to choose from, how does one choose favorites?

First, we have to confess that we have ignored our own warning and succumbed to the temptation to collect real oddballs—pachypodiums, tylecodons, crested mutants, monstrous cultivars—the stranger the better. Most of these are kept in their cages—wonderful grotesqueries too weird to mix well in a landscape setting but marvelous in a sideshow. However, some we have used and they worked out quite well. We will mention a few now and others will be described in more detail in chapter 5.

Low-growing rosettes are found in many genera—*Agave, Aloe, Crassula, Echeveria, Sedum, Tacitus, Yucca,* and others. Colors include nearly white, gray, blue, green, brown, red, and nearly black. To some people they look like thick-petalled roses detached from the bush and placed on the ground. Sizes can range from less than 1 in (2.5 cm) to well over 1 ft (0.3 m). Most are undemanding over a wide range of cultural conditions. Succulents are custom-made foreground plants, superb when set into dark gravel or between rocks (see figures 5-6, 5-8, 5-19, and 5-26). The only thing that can be said against them is that some are too common. But contextualizing them in an uncommon way will freshen appreciation of these beautiful plants. It's an old lesson from the classic masterpieces of Japanese gardens: Common objects in fresh environments can startle us with their beauty.

Strange bush forms abound in the succulents of the genera *Ceropegia*, *Crassula*, *Euphorbia*, *Haworthia*, *Pelargonium*, *Sedum*, *Senecio*, and *Stapelia*, to name but a few (see figures 5-3, 5-4, 5-14, and 5-21). Size and color are so varied that the plants can be used in all sorts of applications. And the character of these wonderful succulents ranges from beautiful to bizarre, from comical to heroic, from modest to spectacular. You can choose from knobby, gnarly, twisted monstrosities or from stiff, straight, upright forms of self-important bearing. They can be bare-bones leafless and naked for most of the year, or well clad with leaves fleshy or thin. The thick leaves can look like beads of jade, stone arrowheads, steel scimitars, or a variety of geometric shapes. Working with these plants is marvelous fun, but sometimes you get the feeling that sculpture is being made out of sculpture.

Then there are the tree forms—or more appropriately, tree deformities—bloated baobabs in miniature. With prickly, spiny, pimply skin stretched to its cracking point over absurdly corpulent trunks; ungainly, awkward, stubby branches organized according to no rules whatsoever; leaves, when they exist, silky smooth and soft or viciously spined and stiff—these plants are absolutely wonderful (see figures 5-5 and 5-17). Their names, such as *Adenium obesum* and *Pachypodium*, give you the idea.

Many are easy to cultivate indoors, but mealybugs are a common scourge. Alcohol and several insecticides are effective as sprays, dips, and soil drenches. Some of our favorite genera are so susceptible that we have never been able to eradicate mealybugs from our collection. *Adenium* and *Pachypodium* are two of these—too bad, because we love them. So we content ourselves with regular sprayings and regular cursings and live with it.

Not all succulents are drylanders, and even among the cacti there are some jungle dwellers that make fine companions for orchids and other tropicals. The orchid cactus (*Epiphyllum*) and Christmas cactus (*Schlumbergera*) are familiar—even too familiar—examples. But there are others that we have found very useful. Drunkard's dream (*Hatiora salicornioides*) is one of these. It looks like a selaginella from a distance, but up close the vernacular name is appropriate—the segmented branches resemble strings of miniature wine bottles (see figures 4-10, 4-12, and 6-3). *Rhipsalis* offers many other epiphytic cacti. We like old man's beard (*R. capilliformis*) and the chain-link *R. paradoxa* (see figures 4-2, 6-3, and 9-17). The second is useful where a bold vine of distinctive appearance is needed.

We have found succulents that serve every indoor landscape, from dryland arrangements to jungle landscapes, from naturalistic designs to the most abstract setups. And their ease of culture makes them a pleasure to work with.

Primitives

(Psilotaceae, Lycopodiaceae, Marchantiaceae, and various families of mosses)

Ornamental genera for indoors: *Lycopodium*, *Psilotum*, and maybe *Marchantia* and various genera of mosses

This is a hodge-podge of primitives that predate the ferns. Whether because of their ancient lineage or their humble beauty, we find them fascinating. Under the glass case conditions mentioned earlier, some are easy to grow, others are easy to maintain but vexing to grow, and others are simply impossible to keep alive. The tropical liverworts (*Marchantia*) are among the easy ones, at least under enough humidity. Our favorites shingle their leaves (thalli, more correctly) across the ground like miniature stacks of moose antlers.

The whisk fern (*Psilotum nudum*) looks like a whisk broom but is a bit more open and a bit more lax depending on the variety (we have several distinctly different unnamed clones). They are a bright, lively green and impart a delicate linear tracery to a design (see figures 4-10, 8-12, and 9-13). They are tolerant of a wide range of light intensity, temperature, and humidity. One of the clones is used as a ground cover in Hawaii and is occasionally mowed! When ours get too tall or too lax, we use shears to top them. This tonsuring does them no harm, physically or visually, and gives us an element of control that makes them even more useful. Their only drawback is that they can be slow to multiply.

We grow many tropical mosses, some on wet soil and others on barely damp soil, all under fair humidity. They seem flexible in their light demands, at least under fluorescent lighting. Some are nearly an inch tall and impart a high-pile-carpet effect, soft and inviting to the touch. Others are of firmer texture and form a mounded surface. The color of most is a brilliant emerald green.

The taxonomy of mosses is in a state of flux, confused and confusing, and we have not made an attempt to identify them. But they are easy enough, beautiful enough, and useful enough to make us believe that they should be offered commercially. These plants may be primitive, but their appearance in the landscape is completely contemporary. However, we usually use the even more reliable fake moss (see page 21).

Other Useful Plants

There are many plants that we underused or entirely ignored but have great potential for use in interior landscapes and deserve mention.

The ponytail palm (*Beaucarnea recurvata*, also known as *Nolina recurvata*) is one of these. It's actually not a palm at all but a member of the agave family (Agavaceae) native to Mexico and Texas. This is hard to believe when you see it grown as a tree in places like southern California. It will reach a height of 30 ft (9 m), with a grotesquely massive, bulbous trunk. The trunk splits into twisting branches, each ending in a shock of leaves like a clump of fountain grass. It's a true curiosity.

Disease- and bug-resistant, tolerant of low light, and very slow growing, it is a popular indoor plant. Confined to a pot, it can be kept at a height of between 1 ft (0.3 m) and 6 ft (1.8 m). Lopping off the top encourages branching but makes the plant even more strange and difficult to mix with other plants. However, we buy them and grow them in tight clumps of juvenile plants, stuffed into a shallow pot. There they remain, looking like a bunch of sprouted onions with lax leaves at less than 1 ft (0.3 m) in height for a long, long time. Still strange, but now a much better candidate for an interior landscape. Here we have used them only once (see figure 9-8).

The genus *Sansevieria* (Agavaceae) is a treasure trove of apt plants for interior landscapes. Related to the agaves and native to the desert regions of South Africa, these plants have long been popular for interior decoration. Given their place of origin, it is surprising that they are so adaptable to different light intensities and levels of humidity. Nearly bug-and disease-free, they are easily grown, though growth is agonizingly slow. They come in a variety of forms, colors, and leaf patterns, which contributes to their popularity. They could be considered too common, but as candidates for interior landscapes with a desert theme, they may be perfect.

Another enormously popular genus in the agave family is *Dracaena*. There are some superb plants here that are well suited to our purposes, and some truly shabby ones that we detest. Among the latter are monstrosities like the corn plant *D. fragrans*. Usually grown to a height of about 6 ft (1.8 m) and then summarily decapitated, it produces a stubby branch or two at the top, each of which bears a shock of leaves resembling those of a proper corn plant. The wound left by the decapitation remains in full sight. Perfectly ugly.

Dracaena marginata, however, is very much a plant for our purpose, although you won't see it used in this series of designs. Grown well (we have seen them close to 10 ft, or

3 m, in height), they are elegant and graceful, a wonderful complement to architecture. Grown poorly, they are an ungainly mess—simply an embarrassment. Unfortunately, it's the embarrassing version that you usually end up with. Growing them well is more a matter of patience and luck than experience and talent. Prune back a wayward branch and what do you get? Usually a mess with one or two new branches taking off from near the cut (not close enough to hide it) and heading off to who knows where. But a pot of several stems grown to a height of 1.5 ft (0.45 m) or so is a dependable asset in a design—looking like a bold colony of grasses if the stems are hidden or a stand of weird palms if they aren't. There are dwarf clones and variegated clones. All are very easy to grow under a wide range of conditions.

Grasses and bamboos offer many tempting possibilities. Bamboos in particular, with their tolerance of shade, seem positioned to make a tremendous contribution. Variety in color, shape, and texture is enormous. They bring a casual, understated elegance to any landscape they grace.

Finally, let us mention a real oddity: *Zamioculcas zamiifolia*. As its name suggests, it looks like a clump of some strange cycad of the genus *Zamia*, although it is not at all related to the cycads. It grows to a height of 3 ft (0.9 m) and its form is strongly architectural. Care is easy, and it tolerates fairly low light in spite of its succulent appearance. It is still little known and underused, but it is becoming more available.

Many more plants could be mentioned as candidates for interior landscapes—far too many to include here. Some of the plants in the interior landscapes pictured in part II are odds and ends whose long-term performance was uncertain but whose interest tempted us to try them. That is just part of the game—trying new things, testing your horticultural skills, and increasing the palette of plants that you can use in an interior landscape.

However, even the most interesting plants will not mask a weak design. They may draw attention away from basic shortcomings in the overall layout, but the distraction is temporary and will soon be seen as a ruse to hide defects in the overall conceptualization of the setup. And seldom does a plant play such a singular role in a design that nothing else can do its job as well. In fact, there is a certain satisfaction to be gained in getting extraordinary effects out of ordinary materials. It's a satisfaction that comes from meeting a challenge and recognizing the deeper attributes of the design.

PART TWO

From Places That Exist to Never-Never Lands: Examples of Interior Landscape Designs

What follows is an annotated portfolio of some of our interior landscapes. Although a few of the pieces are models for larger works, many can stand on their own in the size constructed.

When plants are used, we name them and indicate their position in the piece. Often we discuss a plant's strong points and shortcomings in the application at hand, adding to the more general comments given in chapter 3. Not every plant or component of the infrastructure is discussed in detail.

Except for the epiphytes that grow naturally on branches, all of our living plants are in pots. This has obvious advantages over growing them in the gravel, sand, or mulch at the bottom of the arrangement. Root competition between plants is prevented. Unwanted leaning toward the light can be countered by simply rotating the pot. Plant and pot can be easily removed for pruning, grooming, treatment for disease or insect attack, or replacement. In fact, planting in pots gives you the opportunity to completely rework the plants in the arrangement fairly easily. These benefits outweigh the nuisance of hiding pots in the arrangement when the design calls for it. However, in some of the pieces, the pots are intended to be clearly visible—they play a role in the design.

Taxonomic completeness was not our goal when we assembled the plants for this series of landscapes. We choose plants on the basis of their availability, their ease of culture, and their appearance. In a few cases, the plants could not be identified with any degree of certainty, but if they performed well under our growing conditions and served our design purposes, we used them anyway. We named these plants only as far as our knowledge allowed. For example, figure 4-3 includes what is obviously an aglaonema, but we do not know the species, cross, or variety, so we simply list it as an *Aglaonema* hybrid. For every species, cross, or variety that we used without having a complete identification, there are many readily available similar plants that will do the job at least as well.

If the setup has special temperature, humidity, or lighting requirements, they are mentioned. We also describe what special measures were taken to realize the infrastructure of the arrangement: Sometimes we decided to construct gravel of a certain weight, color, and texture; other times found wood was painted, joined, or sculpted; in some cases stone was painted, joined, or fabricated.

Occasionally, we mention the compositional devices used to create the effect: dim back lights; a sloping ground cover or converging walls to enhance depth; a shadowed foreground to imply more height; multiple plants of the same species placed to lead the eye from one point to another, to hold the composition together visually, and to establish unity; and branches and roots of trees arranged to create the design's flow.

Some of the landscapes are shown in stages of construction—the infrastructure without plants followed by views of the completed project. Occasionally, when there are several examples of the same kind of design, only the infrastructure of some are shown accompanied by a description of how the design can be furnished with plants and completed. Some basic designs are shown in several variations, furnished with different sets of plants. Some arrangements consist only of the infrastructure.

Many of our landscapes are wall pieces. Some hang in front of a wall and others have sections that are directly affixed to a wall. The wall acts as a backdrop and is textured and painted to be an integral part of the composition. Floor space may be at a premium, so the depth of the piece from front to back is shallow in relation to its height. Often the piece has a modular aspect and can be seen as a unit that can be joined to similar units, extending the design to whatever length is needed. Such a design can even be wrapped around corners or interrupted by a door or hallway and continued on the other side.

Some of the wall pieces can be easily modified into freestanding floor pieces to be seen from all sides. Such pieces can function as room partitions. Of course, they can be conceived as two wall pieces placed back-to-back. It is more challenging to design the piece without a separating wall, so that it unfolds in unexpected ways as you walk around it. Such a design comes close to being sculpture in the round. The distinction between architecture, sculpture, and garden design is not always clear, and perhaps it shouldn't be. We enjoy them all and take particular pleasure in seeing them combined with one another.

All of our examples are intended to be seen as landscapes. Some may stretch the point or challenge the conventional notions of landscape. If so, we are happy. Those were some of our goals.

CHAPTER FOUR

FANTASY JUNGLES

*T*he landscapes in this chapter are meant to suggest bits of jungle scenery, vignettes of exotic landscapes where brightly plumaged birds, iridescent butterflies, and spectacular flowers vie for your attention. A jungle is a place of unbridled growth, where a profusion of plant life is primed by an abundance of sun and rain. Here plants luxuriate in the warmth and moisture, unfolding leaves and flowers unmistakably tropical—black patent leather alocasias embossed with chevrons of ivory, begonias of hammered silver or pewter, calatheas in black velvet or shimmering satin patterned like bird feathers or butterfly wings. And the flowers—indescribable and in varieties unimaginable. The orchids alone number more than twenty thousand species. But this glorious profusion is seldom seen in small, concentrated pockets—it is dispersed. Even in a space of a few square miles, the jungle can be a rather monotonous place, a jumble of growth with no apparent structure.

The landscapes featured here are not copies of any we have seen in the wild—not the high mountain jungles of the Peruvian Andes, the lowland forests of Brazil, or the ocean-locked islands of the Caribbean. No jungle that we have visited offers the concentrated diversity seen in our landscapes. The pieces featured here are highly idealized fantasy jungles rather than honest portraits of jungle vignettes.

In fact, in no setup do we restrict ourselves to the plants of a given region or even a given continent. Rather, we mix and match varieties according to the demands of the design. Most of the plants we use are readily available and quite easy to grow. For those that are rare or more difficult to grow, we suggest alternatives that will give the same effect with less trouble.

The overall composition is the most important part of a setup, but in some cases we show off a favorite tropical plant or two. Even so, these specimens are beautiful but not overly ostentatious, and they complement the setting without calling too much attention to themselves.

These pieces are considered jungle landscapes because they communicate a sense of unbridled growth and the moist, warm atmosphere that makes such luxuriance possible. An abundance of water is implied but not actually present. Although the variety of plants in some of our pieces is far greater than usually can be found in jungle areas of the same size, almost all of the particular plants have the appearance of species actually found in the wild.

A GIFT OF TWO JUNGLES

A runoff stream waits to be refreshed by the next downpour; the stones along its bottom are still glistening wet from the last rain. Exotic ferns and other tropical plants have taken hold on the banks of the stream and even on the branches above it. Cloistered away from the water's edge, under the protection of two ancient trees, is a colony of lady slipper orchids.

To what jungles must one travel in order to see these exquisite orchids? Lady slippers are found throughout southeast Asia, Indochina, and northern Malaysia; they are all under the protection of CITES (Convention on International Trade in Endangered Species) and cannot be collected. But the lady slipper pictured in figure 4-1, *Paphiopedilum* Maudiae 'Magnificum' is not to be seen anywhere in the wild. Maudiae is a product of the plant breeder's art, a primary hybrid of *P. callosum* from Thailand and *P. lawrencianum* from Borneo—a gift of two jungles. The cross has been famous for over a hundred years, but you still must reach deep into your pocket to purchase an awarded clone. That's

because paphiopedilums, have resisted propagation by tissue culture, and plants grown from seed are not likely to be as good as the parents. So new plants of the awarded clones are propagated vegetatively by dividing old plants—an infuriatingly slow process, with lady slipper orchids yielding only one or two divisions per year. Yet in spite of its exquisite and exotic appearance, Maudiae is an easy orchid to grow. Light demands are low and normal living room conditions suit it just

fine. It flowers both in spring and fall and each precious blossom lasts from four to five months.

The effectiveness of a landscape should not depend on the choice of plants used to furnish it. In this piece, we could have used other slipper orchids, other orchids, or other plants altogether. But nothing quite matches the cool aloof elegance of this icy green and white treasure.

The stones pictured here are ordinary river pebbles. Waxing them or

coating them with varnish or urethane can make them appear wet. Of course, flowing water could be added to the design. Miniature pumps are available for that purpose and are easy to install.

The wood, found cottonwood, required a minimum of reshaping. In general the pieces of wood were selected to have enough interest to hold their own in the design without stealing the show.

Plants in figure 4-1, clockwise from upper left:
1. *Tillandsia usneoides* Spanish moss (several clumps across top)
2. *Platycerium ellisii*
3. *Codonanthe crassifolia* (2)
4. *Platycerium bifurcatum* 'Dwarf' staghorn fern (upper right)
5. *Brassaia (Schefflera) arboricola* 'Dwarf' (several)
6. *Brassaia (Schefflera) arboricola* 'Variegated Dwarf'
7. *Paphiopedilum* Maudiae 'Magnificum' (several)
8. *Aglaomorpha* or *Drynaria*?
9. *Adiantum raddianum* 'Sea Foam' (several)
10. fake fig tree

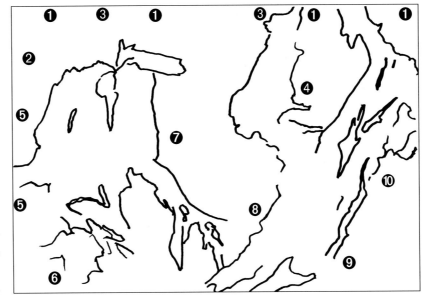

Diagram for 4-1

4-1 The famed slipper orchid Maudiae holds court in a jungle clearing

AFTER THE FIRE

The plantation was within a two-hour drive from Bogota, Colombia. Its sprawling hacienda was surrounded by a patio covered with orchids and other tropicals. The collection continued into the garden, where it surrounded a swimming pool that was fed by a natural waterfall. Ostensibly a farm that earned its keep from crops of coffee and sugarcane, it was the plaything of its gentleman-farmer-politico owner. He spent less than a month out of every year on the place, but it was kept running throughout the year by a retinue of cooks, housekeepers, gardeners, and farmhands.

In touring the estate, we came across a cleared field newly planted in sugarcane. A year before, it had been wild—just a bit of jungle typical of that throughout the region. But all growth had since been cut to the ground, the larger stumps had been uprooted manually, and what would burn had been burned. At the borders of the field, where sugarcane had not been planted, the jungle was coming back.

The parts of trees that had not burned completely had been pushed to the edge of the forest; against their blackened remains, new growth was beginning, like jewelry set off on black velvet. Even after a year in this tropical climate, it was not seedling trees and shrubs that dominated the new growth, but rather nonwoody plants. They had the edge in rate of growth, and they were taking full advantage of the added light. Small gardens had been formed, each under the protection of a half-charred remnant of a tree.

With these chance gardens in mind, we set up the landscape in figure 4-2, trying to capture the contrast between scorched, age-hardened wood and vibrant young plants. The plants, all from our own collection, are for the most part readily available and easy to care for.

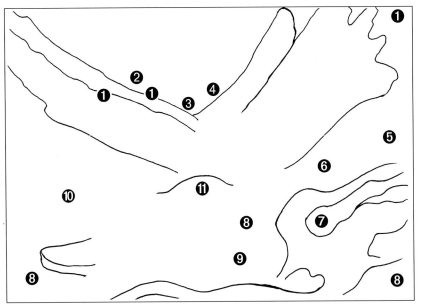

Diagram for 4-2

Plants in figure 4-2:
1. *Tillandsia usneoides* Spanish moss
2. *Neoregelia marmorata*
3. *Rhipsalis capilliformis* old man's beard
4. *Vriesea splendens*
5. *Aglaonema* 'Silver Queen'
6. *Davallia* or *Humata*? hare's-foot fern
7. fake moss
8. *Selaginella kraussiana* 'Aurea'
9. *Cryptanthus fosterianus*
10. *Syngonium* 'Dwarf'
11. *Haemaria discolor* jewel orchid, with two spikes of white flowers

4-2 After the Fire: A new flush of growth

SNAG

Where a tree once stood, only a snag of its trunk remains. In falling, the tree allowed more light to reach the jungle floor. In decaying, it gave back to the soil what it once borrowed for its own growth. Now the tree is the bed of a jungle garden. And that is the effect that we tried to capture in figure 4-3.

Where in the world could you see such a jungle scene? Everywhere and nowhere. Snags and small clearings made by fallen trees are common in forests everywhere. But nowhere will you see this much variety in such a small space, or this particular mix of plants. In fact, some of the plants here are native to South America, while others come from Asia. And some are to be seen only in gardens and greenhouses: They are hybrids by human design. All of the plants used here are easy to grow and easy to find, except for the hybrids (see the source list at the back of the book).

Of course, many other plants could have been used in place of the ones you see here. But there is something quite special about the lady slipper orchid near the center of the arrangement. That slipper orchid is *Paphiopedilum* Papa Rohl, an elegant beauty with a touch of strangeness. The flowers, borne one or two to a stem, are a blend of purple, brown, green, and white. The pouch is veiny, and the petals have warts and hairs. A vigorous grower, it blooms twice a year, and the flowers last for months. Even out of flower, the plant won't embarrass you—its neat habit and its mottled foliage are attractive enough to stand on their own.

Plants in figure 4-3:
1. *Tillandsia usneoides* Spanish moss
2. *Tradescantia multiflora* (also known as *Gibasis geniculata*)
3. *Brassavola nodosa* lady of the night
4. *Aglaonema* hybrid
5. *Begonia* 'Kismet'
6. *Saintpaulia* miniature African violet
7. *Peperomia caperata* 'Emerald Ripple'
8. *Begonia* 'Dewdrop'
9. *Tillandsia streptophylla*
10. *Tillandsia ionantha*
11. *Paphiopedilum* Papa Rohl

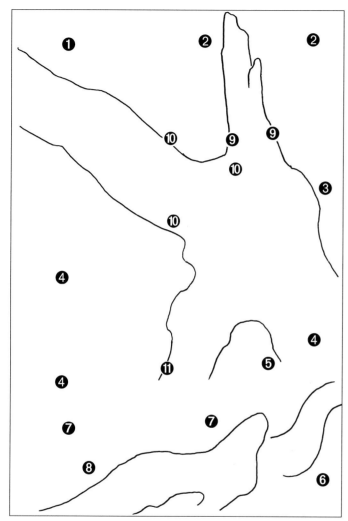

Diagram for 4-3

4-3 Snag: Surrounded by exotic plants

JUNGLE ARBOR

Light is a precious commodity in the jungle, and for the trees and vines that need a great amount of it to survive, it's a mad rush to break through the leafy canopy. But other plants require far less than full sunlight. These are the plants of the understory—the plants that grow on the jungle floor or epiphytically on shrubs and low branches. These are the kinds of plants in figure 4-4.

Formed out of tree roots and branches, an arbor dominates the center of this arrangement. Inside this structure, the red spathes of a dwarf *Anthurium andraeanum* suggest a ritual fire. A corona of exotic plants—ferns and orchids from tropical jungles around the world—surrounds the mouth of the cave. Bark the color of black mahogany covers the ground.

The white orchids are from Madagascar. The one at the top is *Angraecum didieri*; at the bottom is *Angranthes* Grandalena. Adding to their exquisite color and form are long white nectar tubes and thick white zigzag roots—all wonderful design elements. Even the foliage is neat and decorative. They can bloom several times a year and each blossom lasts for weeks. Intensely fragrant in the evening, the scent of a single blossom will permeate an entire room. These glorious orchids grow easily if given humidity in the range of 60 percent to 80 percent, and they will bloom under low light.

The other conspicuous flower is a streptocarpus hybrid. A relative of the African violet, it has the usual faults and strengths associated with that clan: It is nearly everblooming even in low light, but the blooms are short-lived and spent blossoms need to be removed; it is easy to grow, but a magnet for bugs. The violet color of its blossoms is brash to the edge of garish, but it is too small a feature to dominate the piece.

Plants in figure 4-4:
1. *Pyrrosia lingua* 'Obaki'
2. *Tillandsia seleriana*
3. *Davallia* or *Humata*? hare's-foot fern
4. *Streptocarpus* hybrid
5. *Anthurium andraeanum* 'Dwarf'
6. *Nepenthes gracilis*
7. *Angraecum didieri*
8. *Angranthes* Grandalena
9. *Microsorum punctatum* 'Cristatum Compactum'
10. *Pinguicola moranensis* butterwort
11. *Tillandsia usneoides* Spanish moss

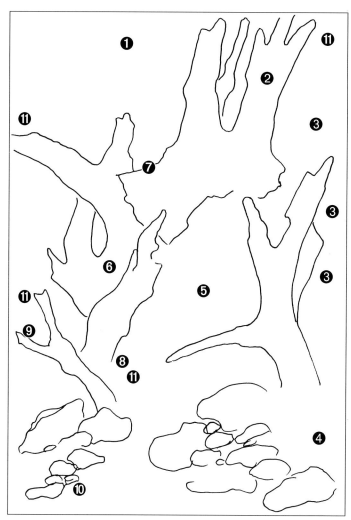

Diagram for 4-4

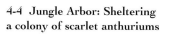

4-4 Jungle Arbor: Sheltering
a colony of scarlet anthuriums

BAOBAB

Even people native to the baobab tree's homeland describe it as a monster, obese, an upside-down-tree! And these are all apt descriptions of the baobab (*Adansonia digitata*) from tropical South Africa. A mature specimen can have a girth of 30 ft (9 m) at a height of a mere 60 ft (18 m).

We have always thought of the tree as a desert dweller, but the recently refurbished Denver Botanic Gardens features a huge concrete replica of a baobab in its tropical conservatory. It currently looks brazenly, abradingly fake, but in the warmth and humidity of the glasshouse, it soon will be covered with moss and epiphytic plants of all sorts: ferns, orchids, bromeliads, gesneriads, and many others. And then it will look more like something that came from nature rather than the cement mixer.

On one of our foraging trips to the local fields, we found a fabulous slab of wood torn from a tree trunk; parts of the roots were still attached. When we turned the slab upside down, it looked like a baobab—or if you squinted and stood back, like Medusa's head. Using this grand slab of upside-down wood, we designed the pieces in figures 4-5 and 4-6.

Seldom do we set up a piece to showcase an object; we made an exception with this piece of wood. However, its form is so striking that we feared it would steal the scene altogether. So we chose our Maligne Canyon panel set as the background. This choice comes close to matching the wood in color and had enough textural interest to deflect a bit of attention away from it. A few strokes of acrylic paint brought the wood to an even closer match. Our Medusa's head-cum-baobab was joined by several other painted pieces of wood to give the design some width (figure 4-6).

We could have completed the design in several ways without the addition of any plants. Stones, from pebble to fist size, could have been painted gray to match the background and arranged at the base of the wood over gray sand. Painting the stones black would also have worked, giving the piece an exciting but controlled bit of contrast at the cost of sacrificing some of its subtlety and mystery. A black background, black stones, and gray sand could have given us another colorless but high-contrast alternative. Instead, we decided to go with a jungle theme, and furnished the setup with plants (figure 4-6).

But we did use this slab of wood again. You can see the piece pictured in figures 9-14 and 9-15 in an even more dominant role.

Many other plants would have worked just as well. A single bold-leafed plant, or maybe two or three, might have been as effective—say, the coppery black-leafed *Alocasia cuprea*, the pewter-colored *A. guttata*, or a bold, black-and-silver-leafed begonia. But the boldness of such plants might blunt the power of the wood forms.

4-5 Boabab; or rather, a large section of a cottonwood bole presented upside down

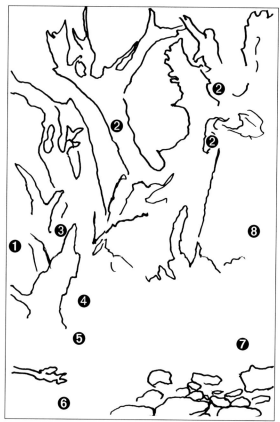

Diagram for 4-6

Plants in figure 4-6, clockwise from upper left:
1. *Aspidistra elatior* 'Milky Way' (barely seen)
2. *Tillandsia butzii* (3 clumps on wood)
3. *Billbergia* 'Fantasia'
4. *Gibasis geniculata* or *Tradescantia multiflora*
5. *Begonia* 'Boston Blackie'
6. fake moss
7. *Calathea makoyana*
8. *Tillandsia cyanea*

4-6 Adding plants to the previous design moderates the harshness

BRANCH FROM AN EPIPHYTIC GARDEN

In the jungles of the tropics, especially those of South America, the trees themselves are gardens—hanging gardens festooned with orchids, ferns, bromeliads, gesneriads, and other epiphytes. These plants of the forest canopy are among the most beautiful of all, and up there in the forest penthouse they get better light and air circulation than they would on the forest floor. When a branch falls from the canopy, it carries its garden with it, and if it falls where there is enough light, the garden will continue to grow.

This is the scenario behind the piece in figure 4-7, in which a fallen branch plays a dominant role in the design. The background, looking like a row of trees, is made up of slabs of cottonwood trunks; behind the slabs is our Maligne Canyon panel set. The three elements—branch, slabs, and panels—have been brought to nearly the same color with a bit of paint.

The log hosts tillandsias, or "air plants." We anchor them to wood or stone with wax or oil-based clay.

Coated wire, stainless steel wire, nylon string, and glue can also be used. There are over 400 species in the tillandsia genus and they are eminently collectable. There are several specialty firms ready to feed the addiction, and any of them can satiate even the most ardent collector (see the source list on page 221).

As we've said before, plants don't make an arrangement any more than clothes make the man. But this setup needed clothes, so we furnished it with plants in our collection—in particular, this marvelous lady slipper orchid, *Paphiopedilum concolor* x *P.* Pinocchio. We couldn't resist showing it off, so we placed it near the center of the arrangement. It's a piece of jade sculpture. When mature and well grown, it can bloom throughout the year. Each spike bears about six buds, which open successively as the spike elongates. Each blossom lasts months, and the entire spike can go on blooming for over a year. The color is luscious—a glowing, translucent light green on opening that later shades to pale yellow. Even out of flower, its neat habit and striking foliage make it an asset that can be used in all sorts of designs.

We explored the possibility of furnishing the branch with many more plants. It did make a more convincing epiphytic garden, but at the cost of obscuring the design of the infrastructure. We thought that the tradeoff was not worth it, so we went back to the simpler arrangement.

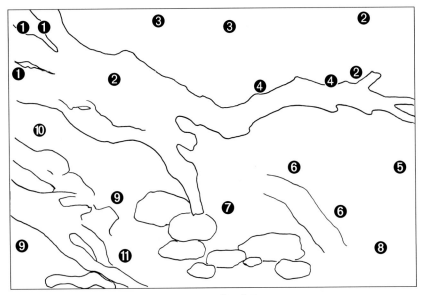

Diagram for 4-7

Plants in figure 4-7:
1. *Tillandsia abidita* (3)
2. *Tillandsia streptophylla*
3. *Tillandsia usneoides* Spanish moss (2 shocks)
4. *Tillandsia ionantha* (several clumps)
5. *Begonia* hybrid
6. *Begonia* 'Granada' (several)
7. *Paphiopedilum concolor* x *P.* Pinocchio
8. *Begonia* 'Guy Savard'
9. *Chlorophytum bichetii*
10. *Ficus pumila* 'Variegata'
11. *Begonia* 'La Paloma'

4-7 **Branch From an Epiphytic Garden**

ROUSSEAU'S JUNGLE

The symbol of the sun high in the sky, the branches reaching for the light, the exotic foliage—we couldn't resist the allusion to the style of the late-nineteenth-early-twentieth-century French painter, Henri Rousseau (figure 4-8). A little stuffed tiger or maybe a giraffe would have clinched the cliché.

We could have used Rousseau-ish plants—plants with more vibrant colors and more striking patterns like *Pleomele* 'Song of India,' with stripes of acid green and insidious yellow; the dumb cane *Dieffenbachia* 'Tropic Snow,' blotched white over blue-green; rex begonias in satiny pink; burgundy coleus neatly bordered in chartreuse; crotons too numerous to name; and all such stuff that makes the eye wince and the stomach churn. Instead we held back and used more modest plants. Not that the plants we used are in any way shabby or likely to go unnoticed. Unlike some of the showy eyepoppers (coleus and crotons, for example), these plants are easy indoors, even under moderate light.

Plants in figure 4-8, clockwise from just to
   the right of middle:
Alocasia x amazonica (largest leaves)
Cryptanthus beuckeri
Begonia 'Granada'
Alocasia 'Black Velvet'
Ceropegia woodii rosary vine (two shocks at
   top)

4-8 Rousseau's Jungle: Living plants of satin, velvet, and silver brocade heighten the surreal aspect of this landscape

JUNGLE SAILING

We don't know how it got there, but there it is—a wooden sailboat with two sails and a crooked mast sitting in a patch of jungle. Maybe it was left behind by Fitzcarraldo, from the movie of the same name. Or was that a motor boat? Of course, what you see in figure 4-9 is not really a sailboat, but it is wooden (cottonwood).

This design came to be as we were moving pieces of wood about, experimenting with various combinations and arrangements with no preconceived design in mind. Other pieces originate in quite different ways. Often we start with a fairly clear idea of what we want the final effect to be, and then we develop a definite plan to get that effect. Often a series of sketches precedes any movement of materials. Sometimes a rough small-scale model is set up as a starter. Other times these various strategies are combined.

With this piece, after deciding on the background and the arrangement of the wood, we waited some time and allowed the infrastructure to suggest, if not dictate, the choice of plants and their placement. It was clear from the beginning that this was going to be a jungle piece, and we chose the plants accordingly. The white Jack-in-the-pulpit-like blossoms of the dwarf spathiphyllum last for months, gradually turning pale green, and the plant flowers throughout the year. The white moth orchid (*Phalaenopsis* hybrid) holds its flowers in perfect condition for half a year and can be encouraged to bloom continuously on the same spike for over a year. And the brilliant yellow-green spikemoss (*Selaginella* species) brings the cool beauty of moss growing on damp rocks to the scene—an effect quite common in nature.

Plants in figure 4-9:
1. fake fig (also on wood, right of center near top)
2. *Tillandsia usneoides* Spanish moss
3. *Begonia* 'Kismet'
4. *Phalaenopsis* hybrid
5. *Spathiphyllum* dwarf
6. *Begonia* 'Dewdrop'
7. *Rhipsalis capilliformis*
8. *Nepenthes ampullaria*
9. *Selaginella kraussiana* 'Aurea'
10. *Tillandsia butzii* (3 clumps on log)
11. *Tillandsia ionantha* (clump on log)

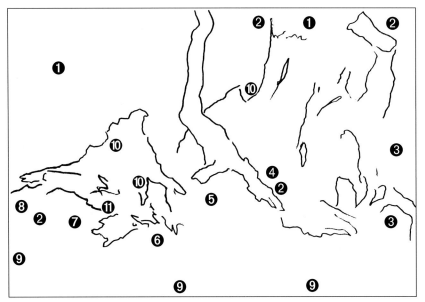

Diagram for 4-9

4-9 Jungle Sailing: Looking like a wooden sloop, the remains of a tree form a backdrop to a bit of jungle

MONTEREY WALL PIECE

California's Monterey Peninsula is renowned for its coastal scenery. Precipitous cliffs drop off into turquoise seas, and perched atop the cliffs or clinging to the sides are Monterey cypress. Sculpted by the wind into fantastic shapes, their trunks and major branches are flattened vertically, the narrow leading edges pointing into the prevailing wind like the prow of a ship. The minor branches and foliage are held horizontally, presenting great sheets of plush green carpet stacked one above the other.

Where the horizontal branches have been pushed flat against the cliffs, nature has created a wall piece on a grand scale, a design that has no focal point and indeterminate ends. The branches are often so long that they seem to be suspended in midair, floating in front of the cliffs. Such a design is perfect to place against an interior wall of a building, and this is what we had in mind when we designed the two pieces that you see here (figures 4-10 and 4-11).

But what warrants its inclusion in this chapter on jungles? The plants we used are jungle plants—because those seen on the Monterey Peninsula are mostly unsuitable for growing indoors. And certainly we have seen cliffs in the tropics with trees and vines espaliered against their faces, supporting all sorts of ferns, orchids, and bromeliads.

Using the same infrastructure, we made two different arrangements. They are somewhat similar in overall effect. One of them (figure 4-10) uses more ferns and fern allies to create a delicate tracery along the branches. The other (figure 4-11) uses tank bromeliads for a bolder look with more contrast.

The architectural aspect of the supporting cinder blocks complemented the arrangement of the wood, so we left the blocks exposed —in fact some were added for the sole purpose of heightening this synergy.

Plants in figure 4-10:
1. *Tillandsia pruinosa* (3 on upper branch on left)
2. *Tillandsia ionantha*
3. *Tillandsia seleriana*
4. *Tillandsia filifolia* (3)
5. *Tillandsia albida*
6. *Codonanthe crassifolia*
7. *Rhipsalis teres*
8. *Hatiora salicornioides* drunkard's dream
9. *Asparagus setaceus*
10. *Tillandsia argentea*
11. *Pinguicula moranensis* (5)
12. *Psilotum nudum* (several)
13. *Microsorum punctatum* 'Grandiceps Compactus'
14. fake moss

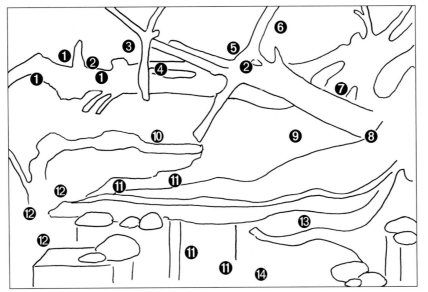

Diagram for 4-10

4-10 Monterey Wall Piece

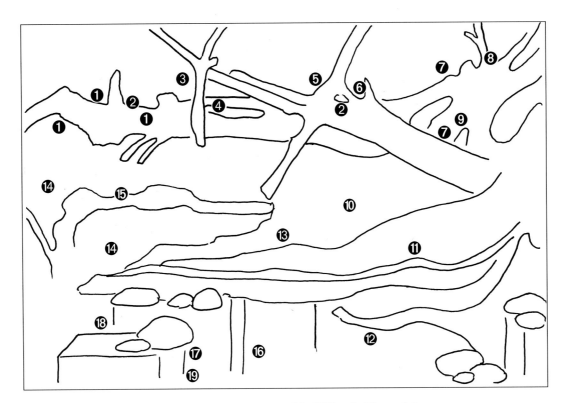

Plants in Figure 4-11:

1. *Tillandsia pruinosa* (3)
2. *Tillandsia ionantha*
3. *Tillandsia seleriana*
4. *Tillandsia filifolia*
5. *Tillandsea albida*
6. *Tillandsia caput-medusae*
7. *Tillandsia streptophylla*
8. *Rhipsalis capilliformis*
9. *Rhipsalis teres*
10. *Billbergia* 'Fantasia'
11. *Neoregelia* hybrid
12. *Vriesea* 'Polonia' (3)
13. *Davalla* species hare's-foot fern
14. *Dendrobium* hybrid (2)
15. *Tillandsia plumosa*
16. *Cryptanthus fosterianus*
17. *Cryptanthus beuckeri*
18. *Cryptanthus* hybrid
19. fake moss

4-11 Monterey Wall Piece II

SOUTH ISLAND, BLACK JUNGLE

From the foot of a glacier, through a rainforest, to lunch on a beach facing the Tasman Sea—all on an easy hike, all in one morning. Where is this possible? On the west side of New Zealand's South Island. These astonishing transitions in topography, flora, and fauna define New Zealand as much as its sheep and hospitable people do. It's an out-of-the-way destination, but where else can you go that offers so much variety, so much wonder, and so much beauty in such a small land mass?

The last two miles of the walk to Franz Josef Glacier is across massive shards of black stone, chips carved from the surrounding rock at an earlier time when the glacier made its way closer to the sea. The subtropical jungle has colonized the walls of the canyon right up to the leading edge of the glacier—white ice, black canyon, green forest—a singular landscape, never to be forgotten.

There are places where you can walk within arm's reach of the canyon walls and look up at hanging gardens where plants have taken hold in the thinnest fissures of the rock. These fissures are fed by the constant runoff of snowmelt from the high country further inland. Lichens, ferns, mosses, and all sorts of higher plants hint at the diversity of flora endemic to New Zealand, diversity on a scale found in few other places.

Figure 4-12, a postcard from South Island, is a piece in homage to the unforgettable scenery we saw there. For the infrastructure, we used our darkest panels, customized black stones and parts of common cottonwood trees.

Plants in figure 4-12:
1. *Brassaia arboricola* 'Variegated Dwarf'
2. *Brassaia arboricola* 'Dwarf'
3. *Hatiora salicornioides* drunkard's dream
4. *Chlorophytum comosum* 'Mandaianum' dwarf airplane plant
5. *Codonanthe crassifolia* (2 shocks)
6. *Brassia arboricola* 'Dwarf' (several)
7. *Microsorum punctatum* (2), unknown cristate dwarf, even smaller and more congested than *M.p.* 'Cristatum Compactum'

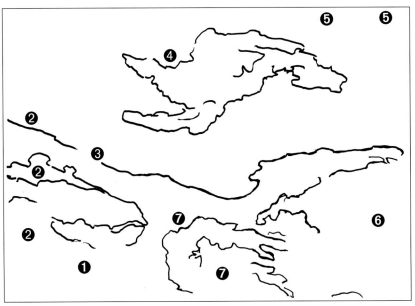

Diagram for 4-12

4-12 South Island, Black Jungle

There are places on the west coast of New Zealand's South Island where the rainforest extends to the Tasman Sea. Over time the action of the sea has changed the topography of the coast: Hills that formerly sloped to meet the water have been reshaped by the waves, leaving a cliff to face the sea.

You can see signs of the process at the crest of these cliffs where large blocks of earth were dislodged and slid to the bottom of the cliff. The forest seeded the mounds that were not washed away, creating a small extension of itself. The new growth knitted the mounds together, stabilizing them and increasing their ability to resist the waves. At low tide, you can walk along the shore and see these small forests pinned against the cliffs. You can view them almost as you would a display in a botanic garden—they are like set pieces, each constructed as something of interest in its own right.

But not every mound is worth a memory. Some seem more like dis-organized heaps of debris—random flotsam tossed up on the shore— rather than one of those lucky arrangements that nature periodically offers solely to please us. But periodically is often enough to fill an afternoon walk with interest and pleasure.

We put together a piece in the spirit of these displaced forest frag-

4-13 Coastal: Cliffs with minotaur rising

ments. The background is much like the color and texture of the cliffs' faces. We tied some cottonwood branches together in a sort of Minotaur-rising configuration and positioned it against the wall. Other branches and the painted black beach pebbles were positioned horizontally to define the base of the piece and delimit its horizontal

extent. Minimalist it may be at this stage, but we already see it as a landscape (figure 4-13).

Figure 4-14 shows the planted version of this setup. We wanted to keep the infrastructure visible, so we used few plants and only plants that are small. All are benign except for one. Remembering the gnats and mosquitoes that are the scourge of South Island and the island's largest carnivores, we couldn't resist hanging a carnivorous pitcher plant (*Nepenthes* hybrid) near the top of the arrangement. There it sits, offering a deadly libation in its flasks, just waiting for one of those blood-suckers to drop in.

Plants in figure 4-14, clockwise from top:
Ficus pumila 'Variegata' (1 suspended, 3 on branch)
Nepenthes hybrid (suspended, upper right)
Chlorophytum bichetii (5)
Selaginella sp. (several)
Cryptanthus hybrids (4)

4-14 Coastal: Cliffs with minotaur rising

RIVERINE

In places where a river's course is fairly deep, seasonal floodwaters can wash the banks clean of plants. Branches, twigs, and even entire trees get swept away by the current and are carried downstream. But in the lazier parts of the flow, in eddies and the inner curves of goosenecks, this litter accumulates and is deposited on the shore. Mud and sand wash onto this beached raft, forming fertile mounds ready for colonization by the surrounding jungle. Seeds are brought in by the animals and the wind. Abundant water and light accelerate growth. And in a few seasons a bit of forest takes hold.

We had this in mind when setting up this piece (figure 4-15). Riverine in concept and riverine in form, the arrangement and shape of the branches suggest the confluence of streams or maybe the pattern left by waves on sand. No great size is implied, and the composition is not seen as a fragment of some larger scene. Rather, it is an entire isolated landscape. The background is a panel that was modeled after a streamside canyon wall in Capitol Reef National Park, Utah. Painted black stones are set at the base of the arrangement, again an idea gleaned from Capitol Reef.

The plants, however, are from the jungles of the tropics, and are far better suited for interior cultivation than those found at Capitol Reef. Again, we kept the plants to a minimum in order to emphasize the rhythm of the infrastructure, in particular the flowing pattern of the branches. (The red twigs are from a little leaf linden; they have not been painted.)

Plants in figure 4-15:
Asplenium nidus 'Curly'
fake moss

4-15 Riverine: A sweep of branches washed up against a canyon wall

CHAPTER FIVE

DESERT
GEOMETRY

5-1 Park Avenue, Arches
National Park, Utah

Opposite:
5-2 Double Arch, Arches
National Park, Utah:
Desert geometry in red

here are deserts other than the Mohave and the Sahara—deserts where there is something to see besides endless stretches of sand. There are deserts born of fire and deserts born of ice. Those born of fire, like the black lava deserts of Hawaii, came into being in a cataclysmic moment. Those born of ice, like some in Colorado, were forged over millions of years by glaciers that carved through rock, pulverizing it, and then deposited the sand in extensive flats amid the eroded rock of ancient mountains. In Utah, giant beds of salt, the residue of ancient seas, were squeezed beneath a vast mantle of stone. The pressure buckled and cracked the mantle, shifting enormous shards of it up through the surface of the earth, where they were shaped by water and windblown sand. Giant sculptures were created—sculptures of limitless shapes, colors, and textures—sculptures unique to the region.

There are places like Bryce Canyon in Utah, where canyon walls have been carved into legions of stone figures standing at attention in closed formation, ready to do battle with the forces that gave them form, the very forces that will eventually destroy them.

There are places like Canyonlands, Utah, where plateaus afford a view of rock formations stretching to the horizon. The gigantic rocks seem to be arranged like buildings along the grand avenues of a city laid out in an unfamiliar but perfect logic. We see the logic in it, we appreciate it—but we don't fully understand it.

There are places like Utah's Monument Valley, where stone monoliths rise from the desert floor like a regatta of giant ships, and Arches National Park, where thousands of arches, bridges, columns, vertical slabs, and other formations exist in such variety that no brief description can be adequate (figures 5-1 and 5-2).

These desert landscapes have several layers of organization. Each layer is in a different scale, and each layer is rich in suggestions for interior landscapes. Even the larger view, when compressed, can be a model for a textured wall or a background. Fragments of the desert scene, a group of monoliths or a series of arches, can offer suggestions for arranging stone or even wood. On a still smaller scale, just a part of a wall or a group of boulders might suggest an entire interior landscape, or at least the start of one. There might be hints for colors and textures, and even the organization of three-dimensional forms.

Some of the desert landscapes that impress us most consist of nothing but sand and stone, and we have designed several interior landscapes that use nothing else. However, plants are a part of most of our desert pieces. There is no more fascinating group of plants than that found growing in the deserts of the world. Again, that's the problem—they are often too fascinating! Every pachypodium is a necessity, every haworthia is a must-have, and every gymnocalcium is to die for; stuff as many on the shelves as possible, spine to spine if need be. Forget about cohesion, composition, contrast, and harmony! Acquire it, cultivate it, and flower it. These are the prerogatives of the collector. And this is the collector's curse in landscape design.

Most of the plants in our setups are common stalwarts of the trade. They are easy to cultivate, slow growing, and have a reliable design effect. Flowering, when it occurs, is just an added perk and in no way debases the design. On the other hand, occasionally we could not resist showing off something really special.

But, as with all of our designs, the botanic interest is quite secondary—all sorts of other plants could have been selected in place of those that were used. Our main concern in these pieces is to evoke the aura of the desert: the restrained colors and the abstract geometry that makes a desert landscape such an apt complement to a modern interior.

NAMIBIA

The Namibian desert is the home of *Euphorbia trigona*, the prominent plant in this arrangement (figure 5-3). Natively, it grows in colonies less dense than you see here, along with a variety of other strange and wonderful succulents. There are no cacti in Africa—cacti are an invention of the Americas—but the spiny, hairy grotesqueries of the Namibian desert are equally fascinating and maybe even more varied in flower and form. After all, cacti belong to a single family, but many families have members that are succulents.

Most of the larger succulents of this region are barrel-shaped, limbless (or have short thorny limbs), and have pewter-colored skin—all adaptations to desert life. Moisture and food are stored in the fat body of the plant; surface area relative to volume is small, which minimizes water loss through evaporation; thorns discourage creatures from

tapping into the plant's body for nutrients and water; and the light skin reflects some of the sun. In this company, the tall, upright, slender *Euphorbia trigona* seems to be an alien—it's a stately presence in a country of misshapen gnomes.

Namibia seems about as fit for human habitation as the moon, and it is a wonder that this barren furnace of a land supports life at all. Raked by sandstorms, scorched and parched by the sun, it offers the fascination of an alien world—a land that has been annealed to an indestructible core. We have never visited Namibia, but photographs of the place are enough to spark the imagination. Often our imagining suggests a design. And we pursue it as

we did here, trying to give the idea substance and make it more tangible.

To suggest the colors of the Namibian desert, we used our Capitol Reef background and staggered the panels to give more depth to the piece. The larger stones were gathered in fields and painted black. The smaller stones, a bit grayer in color, were purchased Mexican river pebbles.

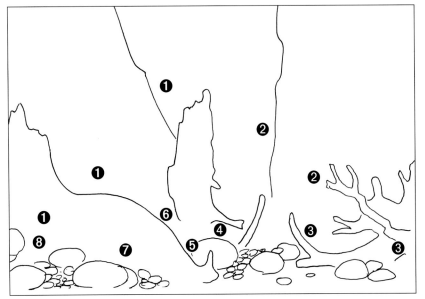

Diagram for 5-3

Plants in figure 5-3:
1. *Euphorbia trigona* (several)
2. *Euphorbia stenoclada* (several)
3. Echeveria hybrid (4)
4. *Lemaireocereus hollianus* organ pipe cactus
5. *Mamillaria fragilis*
6. *Haworthia fasciata*
7. *Crassula marnieriana*
8. *Tacitus bellus* (3)

5-3 Namibia

ARCHEOLOGY

Buried in the desert sands of the Mideast and Africa are the ruins of ancient civilizations. Sometimes entire buildings are unearthed, along with food vessels, furniture, and clothing—all preserved by the dry heat. Occasionally, even the skeletal remains of former inhabitants are brought to the surface. These finds give us some insight into how these cultures survived in such inhospitable and unforgiving terrain.

In our minds, this piece suggests not only an archeological dig, but also a dig on a desert site (figure 5-4). The plants have something to do with that association, but it's the forms and colors that lock it in. There is nothing fancy about the plants—they come from various deserts, mostly in Africa. We have collected all sorts of cacti and other succulents and we love to show them off. However, sometimes less is more, and this may be one of those times.

Notice that this piece and the piece pictured in figure 5-5, a Pack of Pachypodiums, use very similar arrangements of stone. Even the backgrounds are the same—our lacerock panels. Here the background is entire and in the other the panels are separated and staggered. The choice of plants is quite different in each, as are their arrangements. We felt that these differences warranted the inclusion of both, and that comparing the two would give some hint as to how we explore variations on a given theme.

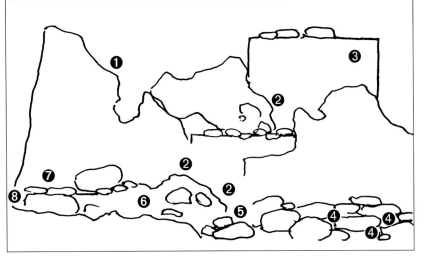

Diagram for 5-4

Plants in figure 5-4:
1. *Crassula argentea* 'Golem'
2. *Crassula perforata* (3)
3. *Rhipsalis paradoxa*
4. *Echeveria hybrid* (3)
5. *Mammillaria fragilis*
6. *Sedum spathulifolium* 'Cape Blanco'
7. *Aloe haworthioides*
8. *Aloe parvula*

5-4 Archeology

A PACK OF PACHYPODIUMS

Four pachypodiums are lounging in the desert, each standing on its one thick, spiny foot (figure 5-5). That's what *pachypodium* means—"thick foot." Although the genus bears a resemblance to the pachyderms, the thick-skinned elephant and its kin, the resemblance is only superficial. The pachypodiums are true desert plants, found only in Madagascar and Africa. Their overall shape is that of a palm tree, pickle, bagpipes, or basketball, and all of them seem to be afflicted by bloat, gout, or general obesity. By current count, there are only thirteen different species, and they are all fit models for Dr. Seuss characters. We love them and would collect every species. But most show their full character only when fully mature, and maturity comes to them very slowly.

The pachypodium used here (*Pachypodium lamerei*) is an exception. Growth is fairly fast, making it relatively inexpensive and readily available. And it seems to have less trouble with that *Pachypodium* scourge: mealybug. It may not be as weirdly wonderful as others in its genus, but it does have a sort of silly stateliness all its own, a form that lends itself to group displays as seen here. And its presence adds an architectural element that is peculiarly unique. Add to this its availability from 1 to 18 ft (0.3 to 5.4 m) in height, and you have the profile of a very useful plant.

Plants in figure 5-5:
1. *Pachypodium lamerei* (4)
2. *Echeveria* hybrid (2)
3. *Euphorbia stenoclada*
4. *Aloe haworthioides* (6)
5. *Echeveria* hybrid (2)
6. *Echeveria* hybrid (4)
7. *Senecio scaposus*
8. *Mammillaria fragilis*
9. *Senecio haworthii*

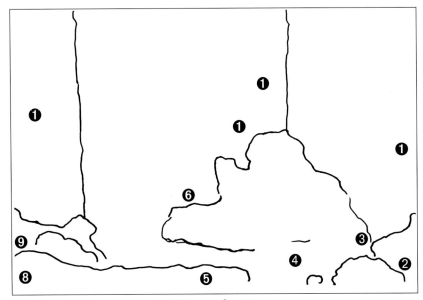

Diagram for 5-5

5-5 A Pack of Pachypodiums

THE DESERT BY MOONLIGHT

One of our most memorable hikes was on the island of Hawaii, on the way to a hilltop where telescopes had been set up. There we would view a new eruption of molten rock and watch the glowing red river flow slowly toward the sea. It was late evening as we made our way across the black lava desert. This was not the smoothly contoured "pillow lava" but rather the sharp-edged craggy sort, the kind that does its best to twist your ankles and tear your boots to shreds. The footing was tricky and the path none too clear. But we could see, scattered about the landscape, plants that were as strange as their surroundings.

Many of the plants were covered with pale gray felt. It is thought that the reflective property of such a coat protects a plant from the searing rays of the desert sun. But on this walk, they reflected the moonlight, looking more like sculptures made of silver or pewter than living plants. It was an unforgettable walk: black sand, silver plants, all eerily aglow in the moonlight. And it was this ghostly landscape that we had in mind when we designed the piece shown in figure 5-7.

Although we have seen it offered commercially, we could not find black pumice gravel, so we manufactured our own (see page 19). Of course, what should be displayed against the black sand is the Hawaiian silver sword plant (*Argyroxiphi-um sandwicense*, see figure 5-6), but that fabulous plant grows much too large, is too difficult to cultivate, and is generally unobtainable. So we substituted *Senecio scaposus*. The wood form is composed of several pieces linked together to form the massive S curve that wends its way up and back through the panels, accentuating both the height and depth of the arrangement.

Plants in figure 5-7, clockwise from mid-left:
The predominant plant—leafless, branching, and flattened green-gray stems with red tips—could not be identified
Aloe? (2 clumps)
Crassula perforata (3)
Senecio scaposus (3)
Agave stricta

5-6 Hawaiian silver sword (*Argyroxiphium sandwicense*), photographed in the only place where it is found natively, Haleakala Crater, Haleakala National Park, on the island of Maui, Hawaii

5-7 The Desert by Moonlight

BLACK DESERT

Figure 5-8 shows another desert-by-moonlight theme. Again, we take as our model the black sand deserts of Hawaii. During the day, the black sand can reach foot-frying temperatures, and few of us can tolerate the ambient heat well enough to fully appreciate this singular landscape. But in the evening, walking in this desert is a pleasure. And if the moon is full, you can easily imagine that you're on another planet. The rock formations take on a phantasmagoric presence, and the plants, glowing pale gray in the moonlight, seem to wander about the landscape like ghosts.

The stone we used in the center of this arrangement looks like lava, but that doesn't say much, because lava is highly varied in texture, color, and form (for example, see figure 5-8). The stone left of center is a fake. We

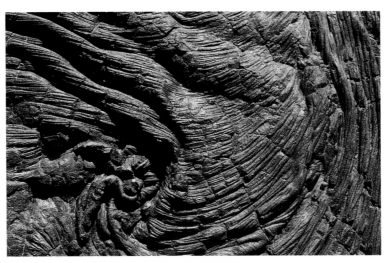

5-8 Pillow lava on the island of Hawaii

5-9 Hawaiian tree fern (Cibotium glaucum), hoary in death, on black pumice in Kilauea Crater, Hawaii Volcanoes National Park, on the island of Hawaii

cast it out of concrete from a mold made of the center stone, and then we painted it to match.

The ground cover, as in our previous piece, is our own made-to-order sand (see page 19). To see how close it comes to the real thing, compare our version to that seen in Kilauea Crater on the island of Hawaii (see figure 5-9).

Plants in figure 5-10, clockwise
   from middle left:
Senecio haworthii
Senecio descoingsii (also far right)
Seyrigia humbertii
Haworthia xiphiophylla (bottom
   right)
Echeveria hybrid (3)
Crassula perforata
Agave stricta
Crassula cornuta

5-10 Black Desert

BLACK DESERT FOREST

Black sand and black cliffs facing the turquoise waters of the Pacific—where else but on Hawaii, Maui, and Oahu (figure 5-11)? The east sides of the islands are much too wet to be considered deserts; but the west sides are more than dry enough. Yet both sides support desert plants—it's that hot, and the black lava sand drains that well. Even on the outskirts of Honolulu, on a hill overlooking the city, a desert garden is being constructed, and a planting of pachypodiums is already in place. Imagine what it will look like in a few years: a desert landscape of bizarre succulents on a tropical island known for its rain-forests.

We had these black sand deserts in mind when we designed this piece (figure 5-12). The main plant in this setup is *Euphorbia trigona*, from the arid regions of Namibia. It is easy to cultivate, and will even grow indoors under moderate light. It's a fairly common plant, available in a range of heights from 1 ft (0.3 m) to nearly 7 ft (2 m). Its tight candelabra branching and narrow upright habit create a strong vertical accent that makes it a perfect candidate for a group planting. Used in this way it forms a strange forest that we can only compare with those we have seen in Saguaro National Park, Arizona.

In place of *Euphorbia trigona* we could have used the very similar *E. lactea* from India. It is even easier to grow and is more commonly available. There is a variegated cultivar that is marvelously patterned in off-white and green. But neither it nor the wild type has the reddish overcast that concentrates in the branch ends of *E. trigona*, a feature that makes this plant more interesting to us.

Plants in figure 5-12, clockwise from lower left:
Senecio haworthii (several, and several far right)
fake moss
Aloe humilis
Euphorbia splendens, crown of thorns
Euphorbia trigona (several)
Echeveria hybrid
Sedum spathulifolium 'Cape Blanco'
Echeveria 'Alpine Rose'

5-11 Crassula weaves its way atop black lava cliffs in Hana, on Hawaii's island of Maui

5-12 **Black Desert Forest**

SNAPSHOTS OF CAPITOL REEF

Capitol Reef in Utah is one of the most recent additions to the National Park system, and it's a great treasure. The park was given its name by early travelers who saw this region as a reef, a barrier to their destination. "Capitol" refers to a white-capped rock formation that reminded some of the nation's capitol building. The park's relative isolation has kept visitation in check, allowing those who do visit the sense of solitude so essential to the desert experience.

This is not a desert of vast stretches of flat, sandy nothingness. This is a region where the earth bucked and buckled to form an enormous stone fold. Then, over a period of more than 60 million years, the elements carved the stone into the grand variety of forms that exist now.

There are a number of superb hikes in the park, but none is more rewarding than the Hidden Canyon Trail. After an ascent of a few hundred feet up the side of a mountain, the trail crosses a ridge and drops down about a dozen feet to the floor of Hidden Canyon. It's an unforget-table landscape. In most of the canyon there are no strong hues. The rock is gray, ranging from near white to near black. You might think that the effect would be somber, but it isn't. Instead, the gray color gives the landscape an impersonal quality that contributes to the feeling of solitude and isolation.

The rock formations in this canyon are not only imposing but wonderfully ornamented as well. The lacerock pattern is frequently seen in many variations, some delicate, some bold, and all marvelous.

Even more startling is the occasional juxtaposition of entirely different rocks: smooth black boulders partly embedded in the gray (or sometimes red) vertical walls. How the black boulders became embedded in the gray sandstone is, of course, a matter of conjecture. But one guess is that a river carried the hard black stones to this site and then deposited them onto the softer gray stone. There, further action of the water gave enough motion to the boulders that they abraded a pocket for themselves in the rock. That is where they sit today, each in its own customized pocket. It's an extraordinary effect. Our Capitol Reef setups began with this theme.

We put together two versions of this piece. The first (figure 5-13) shows only the gray and black rock. The second (figure 5-14) uses the same setup but incorporates desert plants into the design. The first is not incomplete but rather a landscape in its own right. Hidden Canyon certainly has sections that are devoid of plants and others that are not. The planted version may hold additional interest. But the barren landscape, uncompromisingly desolate, is the one we prefer. It's the one that we believe most strongly captures the essential mood of the desert.

Plants in figure 5-14:
1. *Crassula perforata* (3)
2. *Euphorbia tirucallii* (2)
3. *Aloe parvula*
4. *Rhipsalis teres*
5. *Sempervivum 'Alpine Rose'* (3 lower right and 3 lower left)
6. *Adromischus cristatus*
7. *Haworthia fasciata*

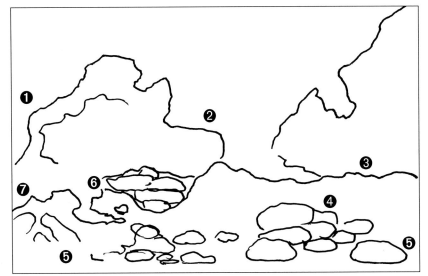

Diagram for 5-14

5-13 Snapshots of Capitol Reef: Rockfall at the base of desert cliffs

5-14 Snapshots of Capitol Reef: At the base of the rockfall, plants gain a foothold

CANYONLANDS FRAGMENT

Canyonlands National Park is a parched, crumpled landscape covering 527 square miles of the Colorado Plateau in Utah. Two great rivers, the Green and Colorado, converge deep in the heart of Canyonlands. But most of the area is a dry, intricate network of convoluted gorges —desolate, forbidding, magnificent.

There is no way of capturing the grandeur of the scene. A photograph from afar reduces it to a pretty texture. Take a closer view and you lose the scale and the scope that gives it its majesty. But walk on a canyon rim. Try to ignore the grand vista spread out below you. Look at the outcroppings of rock. Often at their bases you find arrangements of stone and wood—simple, coarse, elemental—with the character of sogetsu (modern freestyle ikebana), but with more power and directness (figure 5-15). This is what we had in mind when setting up this piece (figure 5-16)—these fragments of the grand landscape, fragments on a more human scale.

Although the stone of Canyonlands appears in a wide variety of colors, some of them menacingly garish due to the heavy metals they contain, we decided to work in the most neutral of grays. This is the color of most of the region, and it's the color that we thought would best capture the spirit of the place— removed, dispassionate, oblivious to human concerns.

The stone we used is lacerock. Lacerock has two surfaces: One, often dark brown or black in color, is highly textured and ornamented; the other is a rather drab gray with few surface features. It is the first side that is usually displayed. But, as with this arrangement, we often prefer the plainer side; it calls less attention to itself and provides a better foil for the other elements of the design.

The background is our erosion panel set (see page 16), in keeping with the color of the rock. We couldn't resist introducing a bit of color with a few plants—after all, the desert is replete with plants that flower extravagantly in high key throughout the spring. In the center of the arrangement is a colony of crown-of-thorns (*Euphorbia splendens*), including some dwarf cultivars. Although spent blossoms have to be removed, their care could not be simpler. In wave after wave, the flowers appear in profusion the entire year, even indoors under moderate light. This photograph caught the colony at its stingiest—in full bloom it's almost embarrassing. They are widely available in a variety of colors: red, white, orange, pink, and yellow. A bit below and to the left of center is the patented cultivar 'Short and Sweet.' Short and sweet it is—dwarf (to 8 in, or 20 cm), very compact, and very floriferous.

Plants in figure 5-16, clockwise from left:
Euphorbia splendens (several); E.s. 'Short and Sweet' (slightly left and below center)
Aloe humilis
Adromischus cristatus
Echeveria hybrid (4)
Gastworthia hybrid? (3)
Sedum spathulifolium 'Cape Blanco'

5-15 Small-scale desert landscape in Canyonlands National Park, Utah

5-16 Canyonlands Fragment: Canyonlands National Park provides a model, but the plants come from several continents

PARK AVENUE

The naming of rocks is a great national sport, and a rock formation has to be truly ordinary not to have a name. Castle Rock, Temple of the Sun, Capitol Dome, Park Avenue—these are all famous features of various parks and allude to structures of human design. Such allusions may be less fanciful and imaginative than those that make reference to people and animals: Twin Owls, the Elephants, Little Dutch Girl, the Three Gossips, and other less politically correct monikers referring to individual physiognomies, random body parts, or perverse entertainments too risqué to describe. Those referring to architecture may be closer to the mark; certainly to us, the rockwork of nature often seems to be architecture on a grand scale, a scale not even remotely realizable by human construction even with today's technology. The formations of the deserts of the American Southwest are some of the grandest and most abstract of all; these are the ones that truly look like architecture.

Park Avenue in Utah's Arches National Park is just such a feature (figure 5-1): a double file of monumental slabs of stone, an avenue of huge skyscrapers rising above the desert floor—as striking a natural analogy of its Big Apple name-sake as one can imagine. We had this magnificent formation in mind when we put together this arrangement (figure 5-17). Of course, trying to capture the grandeur of nature's version would be foolish. But we wanted to suggest the compositional aspects of the rock arrangement and its abstract geometric quality. The challenge was to do so while avoiding the "model railroad syndrome"—a cutesy miniaturization as faithful to the original as possible except for scale. So we greatly simplified the composition and used the simplest materials.

We kept the planting to a minimum and included only desert plants. Many desert plants have an abstract geometric character that complements such a setup. In this case, the bare piece without plants seemed too simple, too austere. Yet even with the plants, the piece is fairly abstract.

Plants in figure 5-17, clockwise from left:
Adenium obesum
Crassula perforata (3)
Tylecodon reticulata
Sempervivum 'Alpine Rose' (several)

5-17 Park Avenue: In stone

MOUNT DESERT ISLAND

There are places in nature where rocks of different kinds and colors come together. It is not clear how this happens, and many different explanations have been put forth to explain it. But the effect is always striking and memorable.

We have seen such places on the west coast of South Island, New Zealand, where black craggy rock rises from pale gray sand against a background of dun-colored cliffs. We also have seen such places on the Hidden Canyon Trail in Capitol Reef National Park, where gray sandstone abuts red sandstone studded with black boulders. But our favorite example is in Acadia National Park, on Mount Desert Island in Maine.

Few coastal areas could have inspired the word desert in Mount Desert Island. Most of the island is clothed in such dense growth that jungle seems a more apt description. But there are places along the beach where black granite rock juts out of the pale gray sand, and in some of these places the scene is backed by gray cliffs. The rock itself is cleaved into rectangular blocks and stacked as though cut at a quarry and then arranged by a master stonemason. The effect, built out of the simplest components, is striking and quite abstract.

In this piece (figure 5-18) we tried to suggest the grandeur of Acadia's coast. We wanted to explore the contrasts and push the abstract element of the landscape theme as far as we could. For the black rocks, we chose slabs of natural slate. The gray "rocks" are just cinderblocks from the local hardware store. The black pots holding the sempervivums are sections of plastic pipe cut to size and fitted with a bottom of nylon screen.

And the plants? There are many superb species endemic to the island and some even venture out onto the black rocks near the shore. But few would survive without a winter dormancy, and none would be convincing as desert plants to furnish this piece.

This piece is not a representation of some specific scene on Mount Desert Island, but the inspiration for the arrangement can be traced directly back to that wonderful landscape.

Plants in figure 5-18, clockwise from upper left:
Euphorbia splendens (2), E. s. 'Short and Sweet' (leftmost)
Aloe humilis
Pedilanthus?
Senecio descoingsii
Agave stricta
Sempervivum 'Alpine Rose' (3 clumps)

5-18 Mount Desert Island: Abstraction of the nearly abstract scenery of Maine's Acadia National Park

TREES IN HIDDEN CANYON

In another section of Hidden Canyon (see page 89), a mixed grove of trees has taken root. In the shelter of the canyon, near the banks of a sometimes-stream, and in the runoff clefts on the canyon wall, trees find a foothold. But even here, growth is slow, and the trees meter out their lives conservatively. When they finally fall, their hard-won wood is preserved for decades, still very much a part of this unforgettable landscape.

In the piece shown in figure 5-19, fallen branches add a less static element to the lace-rock arrangement. (Again, we used the back of the rock rather than the textured front.) The fallen trees are large branches of a cotton-wood—not a species that you would find growing in a desert. But the color is perfect, and their flowing rhythm sets off the static angularity of the stone to good effect. The wall is our Capitol Reef panel set.

Note how the line of echeverias mimics that of the wood but in reverse, giving both contrast and continuity to the design. These "live-fore-vers" are growing here as you would find them in nature, in the fissure of a rock.

The large plants to the left of center are opuntias of some sort. They are weirdly wonderful, and we love them for their architectural form, but hate them for their bugginess. Mealybug and scale became such persistent problems with these plants that we finally abandoned them to the garbage heap.

At the right of the arrangement is *Euphorbia caput-medusae*—and Medusa's head is what it looks like, with a shock of serpentine stems atop a stout, cylindrical stem. This one is easy to grow, and although it isn't insect-proof, it shows considerable resistance and accepts occasional spraying with insecticide without complaint.

Plants in figure 5-19, clockwise from left:
Opuntia? (3) (We do not know the species of this extraordinary plant. Unfortunately, it is a magnet for mealybugs.)
Crassula argentea, jade plant (several small starts)
Sempervivum 'Alpine Rose' (many)
Euphorbia caput-medusae
Monadium stapelloides
Faucaria tuberculosa

5-19 Trees in Hidden Canyon: After a scene in Canyonlands National Park

EDGE OF THE DESERT

Why are we so fascinated by the desert landscape? Surely the stark, clean geometry of its rock forms and their placement has something to do with it. We thought that we could understand and appreciate this singular landscape even more if we abstracted the shapes to their most basic form, successively paring away the inessential elements in the design.

However, each new level of abstraction led us further away from a naturalistic representation of the desert. With the piece shown here (figure 5-20), we felt that the abstraction had brought us to the edge of what one could consider a desert landscape. The forms are so architectural that the piece could be a highly simplified model for a complex of buildings—read the plants as trees and shrubs. Pushing the abstraction further gave us pieces that had to be placed in different chapters. The memorial piece in figure 8-4 is such an example.

To see the present setup as a desert, one has to see the concrete slabs as representing stone slabs like those in Monument Valley. The black stones might be erratics like those in Capitol Reef National Park. The plants, however, need no interpretation whatsoever; they are unmistakably desert plants. With their strange growth patterns, these plants are already sufficiently abstract, and they fit into an abstract desert landscape perfectly.

The plant at the right is *Euphorbia totirama*, named for its twisted stems. What you can't see in the photograph is its base—the twisted stems emerge from a tan, hemispherical mound, a specialized part of its root. When photographed, this structure had a diameter of only 3 in (7.5 cm). But it's still growing, and adding more and more interest to the plant. To prevent the plant from becoming too lanky, you can prune the upper part of the stems away by slicing through them with a sharp knife or razorblade. It's an easy job (wear leather gloves) but messy, as the plant bleeds a lot. This pruning not only reduces the height of the plant but also encourages it to branch, and this usually improves its appearance. The cut ends eventually heal, and the scars are neat enough not to cause any disfiguration. This task needs to be done only every year or so and is effective in controlling the growth of many other succulents with the same sort of branching pattern.

Plants in figure 5-20, left to right:
Euphorbia stenoclada (2)
Crassula perforata (3)
Opuntia 'Maverick'
Euphorbia tortirama

5-20 Edge of the Desert: Where realism borders on abstraction

RED DESERT

Red deserts can be found in the American Southwest—the sand is red and the stone is red. It is iron oxide that gives the landscape its color. Where there are plants, their green, silver, or blue foliage provides enough contrast to push "stunning" to "surreal." In more familiar landscapes, you expect to see flowering plants supplying a bit of red here and there against a mostly green background. But these deserts enact a reversal: it is the desert that is red, and the plants provide the more modest colors, at least when out of bloom.

No matter how many times we see these landscapes they continue to fascinate and excite us. In the pieces in figures 5-21–5-23, we tried to suggest the surreal quality of these red deserts. We did not use the more strident reds that we see in nature, as we thought such color would be too assertive in an architectural setting. We still see these pieces as red deserts, but with some moderation of nature's more wild side.

The tall stone and a few of its companions were not altered in any way. They were found with the patchwork pattern and coloration shown. The others, originally pale gray and buff, were painted to match the first set.

The background, too, was painted to match the color and pattern of the key stone. This added depth to the composition and gave it the suggestion of greater size. Actually, the piece is quite small, about 2 by 3 ft (0.6 by 0.9 m), but it could be interpreted in a much larger scale. This is true of many desert landscapes, both in nature and of human design—seen in a photo, they appear to be much larger than they actually are. The effect has something to do with the clarity of the arrangement and the simplicity of the geometric forms.

The key plant in the arrangement is *Euphorbia stenoclada* from the deserts of Madagascar. It eventually grows to a height of 40 in (about 1 m), but that takes a very long time. A bit of butchery will keep it as small as 1 ft (30 cm). It's a living tangle of barbed wire, a leafless spiny disorganized shrub that some will find hideous, but we love it. Here it creates a textural mass that wraps around much of the design, giving it a sort of thorny unity while sharply contrasting in color, form, and texture with the smooth red rock. Such a piece of work as *E. stenoclada* surely belongs in a desert.

Plants in figure 5-21:
1. *Euphorbia stenoclada* (several)
2. *Haworthia fasciata*
3. *Crassula marnieriana*
4. *Crassula cornuta*
5. *Tacitus bellus* (3)
6. *Aloe?*
7. *Haworthia xiphiophylla*
8. *Agave stricta*

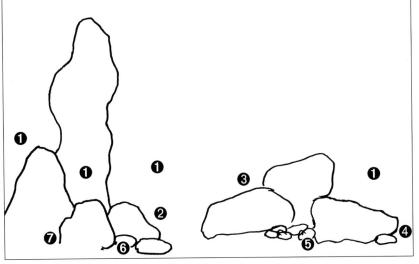

Diagram for 5-21

5-21 Red Desert

RED DESERT II AND III

Some of the most spectacular desert scenery is found in the American Southwest, and we have enjoyed hiking desert trails there for more than a quarter of a century. A camera and a sketchpad are as crucial to us on such trips as are sunscreen and large canteens of water. Even in early spring, the desert is hot, dry, and often dusty—but such discomfort does nothing but emphasize how strange and beautiful this landscape is. It's a landscape not without danger, and it demands your attention and respect. In return it fills your eyes and mind with wondrous beauty.

Red deserts with formations and paths like those pictured in figures 5-22 and 5-23 are not uncommon. But these pieces were not inspired by any one hike, or even by any one desert. Rather, they are amalgams of memories expressed using the materials we had on hand.

In these arrangements, the stones are not only real but also authentic—we collected them in the open desert during one of our trips. Of course, in a larger setup, the stones would be artificial (see page 18).

The background painting and the sand are the same that we used in the first Red Desert (figure 5-21). In each case, the stones that form the path are not stones at all, but rather chunks of tree bark. The texture, color, and size were right, and the material was right at hand.

These two pieces are variations on the same theme, and the same set of stones is used in each. We simply rearranged them. In the first piece (figure 5-22), the stones are positioned to give a strong vertical component to the design; in the second piece (figure 5-23) the emphasis is on the horizontal energy the stones impart. There are many other configurations that would work just as well. That's the nice thing about working with forms as abstract as these—there are so many distinctly different ways of positioning them.

The plants in the design also contribute to the desert theme, although the feathery asparagus fern (*Asparagus setaceus*) that plays the dominant role in the background may give you some pause. In spite of its delicate appearance, it is native to arid regions of South Africa. In the scale seen here, it can be seen as a windblown tree, in a shape not unlike a windswept Monterey cypress. Seemingly fragile, it is actually tough and hardy. The plant has a fine texture like that of many desert plants that have a small leaf surface to minimize water loss by evaporation.

Using *Rhipsalis teres* in these two setups, on the other hand, is a real contrivance. It is a cactus, but it is a South American jungle dweller, and it lives in the trees as an epiphyte, not on the ground as its species name would have you believe. Anyway, it is undemanding and looks convincingly at home in these desert pieces.

Plants in figure 5-22:
1. *Agave stricta*
2. *Rhipsalis teres* (2)
3. *Crassula cornuta* (bottom)
4. *Asparagus setaceus*
5. *Haworthia fasciata*
6. *Haworthia papillosa*
7. *Haworthia xiphiophylla*
8. *Tacitus bellus*

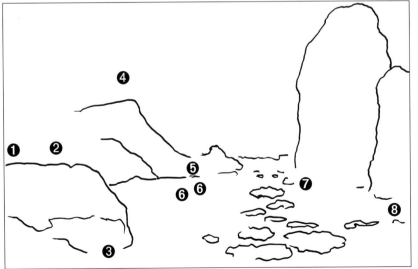

Diagram for 5-22

5-22 **Red Desert II**

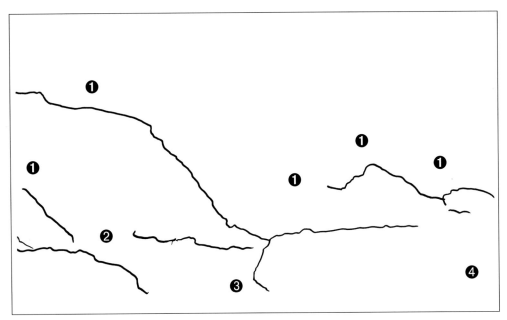

Diagram for 5-23

Plants in figure 5-23:
1. *Asparagus setaceus* (several)
2. *Rhipsalis teres* (2)
3. *Aloe* (several)
4. *Aloe haworthioides*

5-23 Red Desert III

DESERT WALL

A landscape wall is a piece designed to have its width independent of its height and depth. It is designed to span a wall of arbitrary length and even go around corners. Such a design has no focal point and no well-defined ends. Figure 5-24 shows a wall found in nature. Our landscape wall (figure 5-25) has a more desert theme.

The wall is constructed out of lacerock, and the front to rear distance is so slight that even in a large application the rock could be installed on the wall as a veneer. Lacerock varies enormously from piece to piece. Its color can be pale gray like concrete, different shades of brown, or nearly black. Patches of yellow or orange lichen often add color to the scheme. Usually there are pockets in the rock, and these make perfect plant pots. Used in this way, a wall of lacerock becomes a vertical garden.

Most of the lacerock available comes from the deserts of Arizona and Utah. We have seen some magnificent examples of it in Capitol

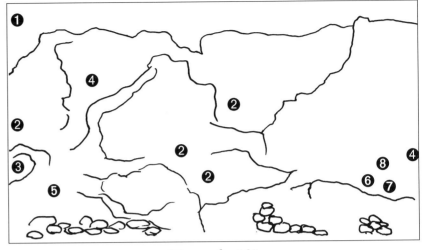

Diagram for 5-25

Reef National Park and in Arches National Park. The sight of it in the wild never fails to astonish us with its unique, rugged beauty. This rock is widely available and it is now a popular design element for outdoor gardens. It is also in high demand for aquarium design.

A lacerock wall can be furnished with all sorts of plants, particularly epiphytics such as orchids, bromeliads, and some ferns. But given its appearance and origin, desert plants seem especially well suited for it. And most are easily grown and commonly available.

Plants in figure 5-25:
1. *Opuntia* 'Golem' (farthest left, top)
2. *Senecio haworthii* (2 farthest left and 3 middle)
3. *Aloe?* (3 farthest left and two others nearby)
4. *Crassula perforata* (left middle and lower right)
5. *Aloe haworthioides* (left lower)
6. *Haworthia fasciata* (lower right, horizontal stripes)
7. *Faucaria tuberculosa* (clump of 3 lower right)
8. *Gasteria verrucosa* (lower right, long, spotted leaves)

5-24 Rock wall and crassulas, Point Lobos State Park, California

5-25 Desert Wall

DESERT WALL II

Figure 5-26 shows a close-up of a portion of our desert wall, reworked a bit by removing a few stones, adding some branches, and exchanging some of the plants. Even a small section of a wall such as this can hold an impressive collection of plants. And the verti-cal layout makes it very easy to view the plants closely. So while the infrastructure might show little change from section to section, the plants can pro-vide enough variety to hold viewers' interest as they walk along the length of the installa-tion.

A long, blank wall can make a prison out of a room. Or it can be transformed into a stone relief supporting a tapestry of fascinating desert plants. Unfortunately, it is the first approach that is almost always used. What a boring waste of space.

Plants in figure 5-26:
1. *Senecio haworthii* (3 left)
2. *Opuntia* 'Golem' (left)
3. *Agave stricta* (upper middle)
4. *Tylecodon reticulata* (middle)
5. *Sempervivum* 'Alpine Rose' (several middle)
6. *Tacitus bellus* (lower right, in flower)

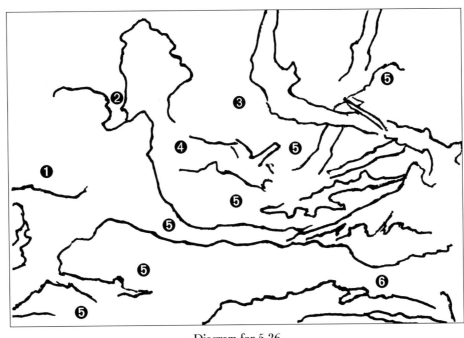

Diagram for 5-26

5-26 Desert Wall II

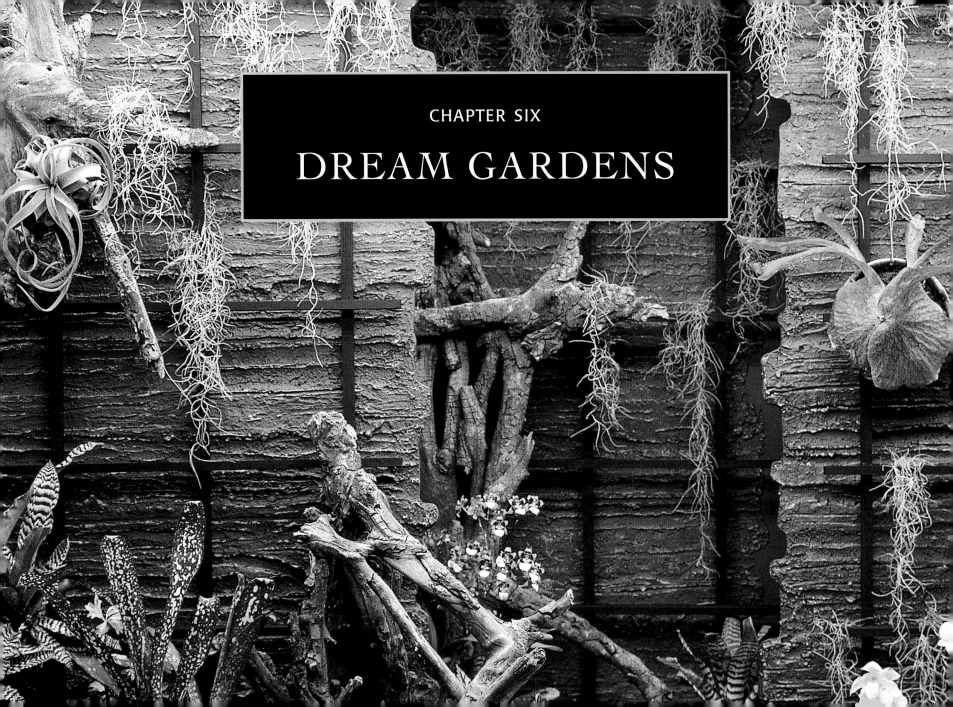

CHAPTER SIX

DREAM GARDENS

These are scenes meant to conjure up tropical gardens, exotic gardens, romantic gardens, gardens where honey creepers search for nectar in the blooms of hibiscus and golden marmosets play among the branches of frangipani. Exquisite plants found only in the tropics would grace these gardens, and orchids in particular would flaunt their matchless beauty. The scent of gardenias would fill the air and linger well into the evening.

No one will mistake the pieces in this chapter for fragments of wild landscapes. These designs are more formal than freeform, and the human hand is evident in their composition. The nonliving components are often of industrial origin, clearly manufactured. As usual, we chose plants that we thought were most suitable for the piece without restricting ourselves to those from a particular region. Even more liberty was taken in the choice of plants for the setups seen here: We did not limit ourselves to those that resemble naturally found species, and when appropriate we used more flamboyant varieties clearly of garden origin.

In these designs space is extended by a number of visual devices that suggest much greater depth than the piece actually occupies. This virtual depth is structured so that the viewer's eye is coaxed along implied paths to explore secret corners of the garden. Staggering planes from the front to the back of the composition creates the illusion. Parts of all the planes can be seen at once from any viewpoint in front of the piece, but only the foremost can be seen in their entirety. The others come more or less into view as the viewer changes position. Some of these planes are established by opaque panels; others by trellises or lattices. The use of opaque panels lends a bit of mystery to the scene: What exactly is it that is hidden behind them? The lattices provide a more open view of the background, but with enough obstruction to toy with the viewer's direct gaze. These devices lead to a rather tight but complicated composition that holds interest over a long time.

The panels and lattices also function as supports for various epiphytics and plants in hanging pots. This allows the design to be carried upward without taking up too much lateral space: Relatively small plants can be used in a space much more shallow than that a tree of the same height would occupy. This approach, which allows the designer to compose smaller elements into a satisfying whole, is likely to be more interesting and challenging to both the viewer and the designer than the usual boring solution of placing a large potted tree in the same space.

There is another advantage to using panels—they make the design remarkably responsive to the angle of the light falling on it. The mood of the piece changes dramatically as the position of the light changes. Lit from behind, the piece becomes a moonlit garden. Place the light directly overhead, and it's a garden bathed in the sultry light of noon. The contrasts are wonderfully evocative, and one might play into this by shifting the light during the day to various positions on a preset schedule. However, we chose to photograph these pieces under lighting that emphasizes their structure rather than the various moods they can evoke.

SPATIAL CALLIGRAPHY

Roots and branches hang from an unpainted wooden lattice and run together to form a mysterious message in forest calligraphy. Or maybe the roots and branches represent Chinese acrobats caught in midflight. Maybe the entire piece is a three-dimensional billboard, a calligraphic advertisement announcing an upcoming performance.

Whatever the interpretation is, the piece does imply motion, maybe even acrobatic motion—hand-to-hand handstands, cartwheels, and somersaults. The spirit of the piece is light and exuberant. There's a touch of the carnival atmosphere about it.

We offer two views of this arrangement, the first (figure 6-1) without plants, the second (figure 6-2) with plants. A glance at the first photograph seems to belie the claim that it's plantless, but plantless it is. That green leafy thing is a silk fig and consequently doesn't count as a real plant. However, even the second version uses only a few plants. This keeps the effect light and open and does not obscure the calligraphic structure. We don't prefer one more than the other and we would let the setting dictate the choice.

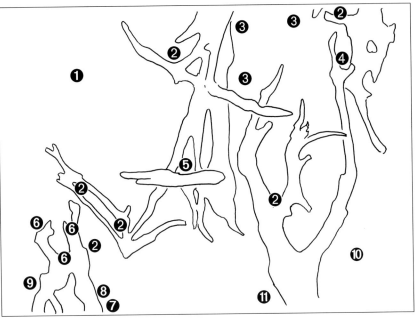

Diagram for 6-2

6-1 Spatial Calligraphy

Plants in figure 6-2:
1. fake fig
2. *Tillandsia ionantha* (6 clusters)
3. *Tillandsia araujei* (3 shocks)
4. *Tillandsia filifolia*
5. *Tillandsia juncea*
6. *Tillandsia pruinosa* (3)
7. *Tillandsia streptophylla*
8. *Aechmea chantinii* 'Dwarf'
9. *Begonia* 'Kismet'
10. *Polyscias fruticosa* 'Dwarf'
11. *Tradescantia multiflora*

6-2 Spatial Calligraphy (with plants)

SENTINELS AT THE GARDEN GATE

We had lunch in a most unusual restaurant in Campinas, Brazil. The building was small: a bar, a half-open kitchen, and six or so tables. But surrounding the building was an extensive open-air patio. A system of thin walls, perhaps 4 in (10 cm) thick by 6 ft (1.8 m) tall, partitioned the patio into a maze of private dining areas connected by corridors. Although there were no doors and waiters had easy access to the rooms, the diners enjoyed the privacy of their own space. Since the entrance to each room was not direct but required a turn or two, diners looking toward the entrance would see a staggered sequence of walls, and only the occasional appearance of the waiter would disturb the view.

Plants in pots were perched atop the walls and cascaded down the sides. The pots must have been secured in place to prevent them from toppling, but we don't know how. Epiphytic plants, some with sphagnum moss wrapped around their roots, were mounted directly to the sides of the walls. More plants were in decorative pots on the floor. And at each turn of the entrance-way, the visitor was greeted by a piece of statuary in ersatz marble: Pan complete with pipes, Leda with her overly amorous swan, or Cupid with bow drawn to target the patron. Kitsch aside, it was all wonderfully done—a complex of small, walled gardens, each with its own individual appeal but having enough in common with the others to give a logical unity to the entire suite.

Perhaps it was the view from one of these dining areas that we had in mind when we designed this piece (figures 6-3 and 6-4). Three trellised panels organize the space. The panels are from our lacerock background. The unpainted wooden trellises were purchased at a garden center and cut to size. Wood rot presents no problem in this application because drainage is excellent and the wood dries rapidly after the plants are watered. Of course, if rot is a concern the wood can be protected by any one of many coatings that would leave the color unchanged and would not harm the plants (see chapter 2).

We substituted pieces of field wood for the statuary, choosing wood that was well-weathered and a bit gnarly. These are our sentinels. But they are friendly sentinels, and they are here to welcome visitors, not to turn them away. They might even be of some assistance in guiding the eye through the partitions and back into the garden.

We outfitted this infrastructure in two different ways. In the first (figure 6-3) we used tropical plants to furnish the piece, giving it the look of an exotic garden, perhaps a small courtyard garden in Brazil. The plant you see in the center of the composition is one of our favorites. It's an epiphytic fern from Angola, one of the staghorn ferns, *Platycerium elephantotis*. Its vernacular name is "elephant ears" or "cabbage fern." This is a baby; when mature it will occupy a space 6 ft (1.8 m) in diameter, a magnificent feature for a landscape large and powerful enough not to be overwhelmed by it. The relatively smaller platycerium perched to the left is *P. ellisii*, and it will reach a diameter of about 16 in (40 cm).

The slipper orchid below and to the right of center is *Paphiopedilum sukhakulii*, a remarkably vigorous, easily grown species that flowers twice a year with blossoms lasting for months. The one here is a particularly fine specimen from the mating of two awarded parents, 'Muscles' and 'Elizabeth.' We can see 'Muscles' in the outstretched hairy macho arms (actually only petals) — but 'Elizabeth'? Beautiful it's not; strange and wonderful it is. It's an eye-catching peculiar presence in bloom and quite attractive out of bloom.

Plants in figure 6-3:
1. *Platycerium ellisii*
2. *Codonanthe crassifolia* (2 shocks)
3. *Platycerium elephantotis*
4. *Rhipsalis paradoxa* (2 shocks)
5. *Hatiora salicornioides* drunkard's dream (2 clumps)
6. *Ficus pumila* 'Variegata' (2)
7. *Paphiopedilum sukhakulii*
8. *Miltonidium* Cleo's Pride
9. *Selaginella*? (several)
10. *Aglaomorpha* or *Drynaria*? (2)
11. *Dendrobium* hybrid
12. *Adiantum raddianum* 'Pacific Maid'
13. fake moss (several)

In the second version (figure 6-4), we see the piece as an autumn garden. There are no living plants — just a few dried sprigs of bamboo and a few branches of nannyberry viburnum painted off-white. Maybe nothing more is needed. It's not the flamboyant aspect of autumn with foliage set afire in incandescent colors, but rather the quieter, more controlled hues of the final weeks of the season.

The second version is as season-specific as the first is seasonless — tropical plants do not experience the change in day length that plants from the temperate regions do, although they may be attuned to changes in moisture. We could have furnished this setup in a spring theme or a summer theme. A winter treatment is another matter. These possibilities suggest that this piece could have been included in chapter 7. But to us, it looks like a garden, and so you see it here.

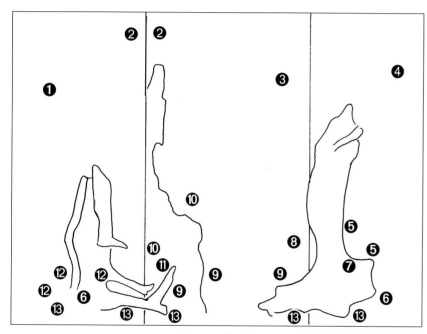

Diagram for 6-3

6-3 Sentinels at the Garden Gate: Slabs of tree trunks

6-4 Autumn variation

MONDRIAN'S GARDEN

With this piece, we wanted to create an illusion of great depth without encroaching into the room more than a few feet. Often we use a succession of staggered panels to achieve this effect. Here (figures 6-5 and 6-6) we thought of amplifying the illusion by opening up the panels, using lattices instead of solid planes. This would allow you to see back through the piece, plane to plane, which would give the appearance of greater depth. But to our surprise, it did not work out that way.

In fact, from a distance, this device caused the planes to compress, confusing front with back. So great was the illusion of compression that three-dimensional character was lost, and the piece appeared more like a Mondrian painting on a flat canvas. Nevertheless, it did give us a design of considerable complexity and a support on which to hang and arrange many plants; features that contribute long-term interest to the piece. So we were simultaneously surprised, disap-

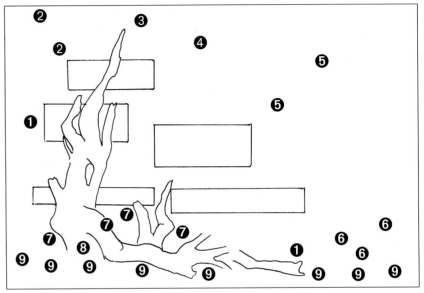

Diagram for 6-6

6-5 Mondrian's Garden: An arrangement in three dimensions

pointed, and pleased by the result.

We should point out that the two-dimensional illusion is seen only at a distance. Close up, the piece does appear to have considerable depth, and walking from one side to the other in front of the piece gives you a succession of dramatically different views of the piece, an effect somewhat akin to that of a painting by Yakov Agam.

Plants in figure 6-6:
1. *Ficus pumila* 'Variegata' (2 mid-left and lower right)
2. *Codonanthe crassifolia* (2)
3. *Rhipsalis paradoxa*
4. *Platycerium ellisii*
5. *Platycerium elephantotis*
6. *Aglaomorpha* or *Drynaria* (3)
7. *Chlorophytum bichetii* (several)
8. *Selaginella* species?
9. fake moss (several)

6-6 Mondrian's Garden (with plants)

ROLI'S GARDEN

Travel into the mountains anywhere near Santiago, Chile, and you will see eucalyptus everywhere. Fast-growing, tenacious, and wildly fertile, eucalyptus has usurped the land. Nothing can compete with it. Even the understory of a eucalyptus forest is barren. It's not just the shade they cast, but the litter they create. It is known that some species actually poison the soil around them—their detritus produces a potent herbicide. So a eucalyptus forest is a monoculture; they tolerate nothing else in their domain.

Chile is not the only country being devoured by eucalyptus. It has run roughshod over vast acreages in other South American countries, divesting great forests of all their native treasures and poisoning the land against any resettlement except by their own kind. How did they come to South Amer-

ica? Who planted them over such enormous regions? Why were they allowed to spread unchecked even in light of the devastation they wreak? No one we have asked seems to know, and no one seems to care.

It's true that Eucalyptus holds many beautiful and useful species. And it's true that many are fire-resistant, and reforesting a burned area with them practically guarantees that fire will not be a concern in the future. It's true that they are fast-growing enough to thwart all competition, and that they are fecund in the extreme, seeding themselves about with unchecked efficiency. They have all the advantages of a shortsighted quick fix, with profoundly tragic long-term consequences.

Even today, the trees are commonly planted in gardens: as wind-

breaks; as ornamentals for their beautiful bark, fragrance, habit, or flowers; and as serviceable crop trees yielding hard, durable, rot-resistant wood for construction and fences. Such was the plan of our late friend and colleague Rolando Chuaqué, whose small grove of eucalyptus at the rear of his property in the suburbs of Santiago flourished in the Mediterraneanlike climate. He routinely cut down trees for firewood and fencing, but the grove would renew itself annually, and annually would stake out a few more square feet of territory for itself. Even strictly managed, the advance was inexorable.

Roli fenced his gardens with the trunks of his trees—he felled them and sawed them into slabs about 1.5 ft (0.45 m) wide and 6 ft (1.8 m) tall. The inner pieces were discarded, and only the slabs with bark were

kept. These became the vertical slats of an extremely durable, attractive garden fence. Against this fence his gardener placed branches and slabs of wood. Plants were set in the ground and others were hung from the fence in pots. We sometimes had breakfast in this garden, sometimes lunch, and always an afternoon snack.

This piece is in remembrance of Roli and the pleasant times we spent enjoying his hospitality and garden. We used slabs of cottonwood instead of eucalyptus. Once the bark is removed from the cottonwood, the smooth surface streaked gray and tan is a fairly good approximation. We set the slabs close together to give the suggestion of a fence. Staggering a few slabs gave us some depth and allowed plants to be placed partly hidden behind some slabs and in front of others.

We used this infrastructure in two variations. In each we kept the planting simple and used only a few species, all of them reliable and readily available. In the first variation, we used the jewel orchid *Haemaria discolor* for the center of the arrangement—it's the one with the gold-striped black leaves and spikes of white flowers. In spite of its almost weedlike rate of growth, it is often sold at florists' shops at a ridiculously high price. It's a shade lover, and we have grown it in houseplant potting mix, long-fibered sphagnum moss, and straight peat moss. In each medium it behaved like a weed, requiring division and repotting every six months, about the same care allotted to our begonias. Were it larger, it would warrant the thug status of eucalyptus. The airy clump in the middle foreground is dried and dyed baby's breath (*Gypsophila paniculata*), available at most crafts stores.

The second version is even bolder and simpler. The orchids and baby's breath have been replaced by bromeliads, and these have a presence even when not in flower.

Plants in figure 6-7:
1. *Tillandsia usneoides* Spanish moss
2. *Pyrrosia lingua* 'Obaki' (barely visible at the top)
3. *Tillandsia juncea*
4. *Microsorum punctatum* 'Cristatum' (lower right)
5. *Microsorum punctatum* 'Cristatum Dwarf' (lower right)
6. *Gypsophila paniculata*, dried and dyed
7. *Haemaria discolor* jewel orchid
8. *Begonia* 'Kismet'
9. *Brassaia arboricola* (several)
10. fake moss

Plants in figure 6-8, left to right:
Asplenium nidus 'Curly' curly bird's nest
Tillandsia cyanea
Billbergia 'Fantasia'
Calathea makoyana, dwarf and compact form

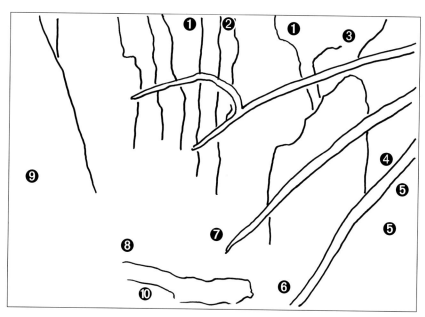

Diagram for 6-7

6-7 Roli's Garden: A garden fenced by eucalyptus slabs in the suburbs of Santiago, Chile, was the model for this piece

6-8 Roli's Garden (variation)

IN A JAPANESE GARDEN

In the classic Japanese garden, strong color is used sparingly and with caution. Control, restraint, and understatement are the guiding principles. A bed of roses would be out of place; a border of perennials in billowing full bloom, not wanted; a bank of azaleas, maybe, but pruned for shape and not flower production. But occasionally, a bright note of color is introduced into a Japanese garden: a red banner at the entrance, a red bridge over a stream, or a red tori in a pond. Seldom is a color other than red used.

Although contemporary Japanese gardens are more abstract and bolder in their use of color, the tradition of restraint continues. The Japanese garden is still an idealization of nature, a place of serenity and meditation.

Ikebana, the art of flower arranging, also has a long and honored tradition. But even within the strict compositional canons of the past, the use of color was always encouraged. In sogetsu, the modern freeform style of the art, the use of color is even more audacious. But once again, red is the most frequently seen high note.

The piece shown here (figure 6-9) can be seen as a hybrid, combining elements of both ikebana and Japanese courtyard gardens. More formal than most gardens, freer and much larger than most works of ikebana, the compromise is in line with the purpose of the piece: It was designed to be an interior landscape. It's more about form and color, and it alludes to no particular garden and no particular place.

Plants in figure 6-9, clockwise from upper
   left:
fake fig
Pyrrosia lingua 'Obaki'
Ficus pumila 'Variegata'
fake moss (several)
Selaginella? (several, and also on lower left)
Haemaria discolor jewel orchid

6-9 In a Japanese Garden

EVENING GARDEN

Evening is the time to enjoy a tropical garden. A garden takes on a special mystical quality after the sun sets. Pale yellow flowers and white flowers seem to glow in the dim light. And many tropical blossoms are fragrant only after sunset.

This piece (figure 6-10) is meant to suggest an evening garden. We used one of our darker backgrounds to suggest the time of day, and staggered the panels to give the piece depth. The black lattice not only gives us something to hang our plants on, but also sets a linear pattern against the panels—a nice geometric contrast with the more organic components of the piece.

This piece is highly sensitive to the placement of the lights. We photographed it using our standard light placement, but lit from behind it takes on a much more mysterious atmosphere. However, it would be interesting to have this piece lit by lights that move automatically to various positions according to a preset program.

Three orchids are used here. On the left, several unnamed small

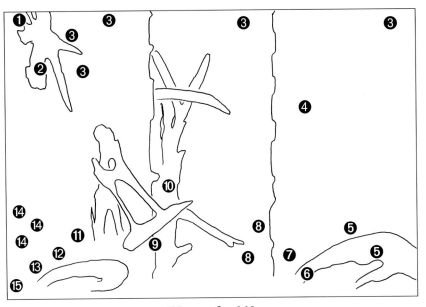

Diagram for 6-10

white dendrobiums with red lips show up strongly against the dark background. These *dendrobium* hybrids bloom twice a year, and each time the flowers last for months. Cultivation is easy, given enough light and humidity.

Closer to the center is a superb hybrid lady-slipper orchid, *Paphiopedilum* Ron Williamson. The flowers are pale yellow when they open, and then gradually turn creamy white.

We have had them last in perfect condition for two months or more. The plant habit is neatly compact, and the mottled foliage is attractive in its own right. Fairly easy to grow, it requires a little more humidity than African violets, but otherwise care is similar.

The third gem of this trio is the complex hybrid *Miltonidium* Cleo's Pride. Its maroon-spotted, pale green flowers also last for months,

and a well-grown plant can bloom twice a year.

These are three of our favorite orchids, and we couldn't resist showing them off. But the design of the infrastructure is strong enough to be effective with all sorts of substitutes. There are many ways to furnish an evening garden. It all depends on how romantic you want to be.

Plants in figure 6-10:
1. *Tillandsia plumosa*
2. *Tillandsia streptophylla*
3. *Tillandsia usneoides* Spanish moss (many shocks)
4. *Platycerium grande*, young plant
5. *Dendrobium* hybrid (2)
6. *Begonia* 'Kismet'
7. *Paphiopedilum* Ron Williamson
8. *Aechmea chantinii* 'Dwarf' (2)
9. *Begonia* 'Guy Savard'
10. *Miltonidium* Cleo's Pride
11. *Billbergia* hybrid
12. *Brassaia arboricola* 'Variegated Dwarf'
13. *Begonia* 'Dewdrop'
14. *Cryptanthus fosterianus* (3)
15. *Ficus pumila* 'Variegata'

6-10 Evening Garden

WALLED COURTYARD

Imagine a narrow walled courtyard in the tropics. The wall is made of stucco, and its pale neutral color is the perfect foil to show off a fine collection of exotic plants: alocasias, anthuriums, begonias, calathias, philodendrons, and other gems of the tropical rain forests. The leaves are so outrageously gorgeous that one might wonder if they were designed by an eccentric artist, but this art is the work of nature, and nowhere but in the tropics does she design plants whose leaves have such extravagant colors, shapes, and patterns.

Without plants, a stucco wall can turn a courtyard into a prison yard —cold, closed, and somber. But bring in potted plants, arrange them against the wall, elevate some on stands to give the composition some height, and hang a few others from hooks placed directly in the wall, and the courtyard becomes an inviting landscape. True, a bit of walking

area has been sacrificed, but the courtyard has been transformed into a garden, friendly and inviting. We have visited gardens like this in Brazil, Colombia, and the Caribbean, and we were always enthralled by them.

Here (figure 6-11), in our interpretation of this kind of landscape, we have used our Capitol Reef panels in the same staggered configuration seen in figures 5-3, 6-9, and 8-15. But the character of each piece is quite distinct. The difference lies in the choice of plants and the way that they are arranged: The first piece suggests a desert canyon, the second a Japanese garden, this one a walled garden, and the last a small sanctuary.

With few exceptions, the plants used here, or suitable substitutes, can be found at any garden center or florist shop, and these days in most hardware stores and supermarkets. These are plants of the jungle understory and consequently require little light and little fertilizer. In general, they are easy to care for, and those that are more demanding are cheap and easily replaced. So not much is needed to set up and maintain an indoor courtyard garden such as this.

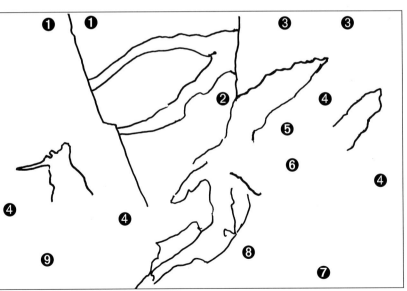

Diagram for 6-11

Plants in figure 6-11:
1. *Rhipsalis paradoxa*
2. *Clorophytum comosum* 'Mandaianum'
3. *Codonanthe crassifolia*
4. *Brassaia arboricola* 'Dwarf' (several right, lower middle, lower left)
5. *Begonia* 'Kismet'
6. *Begonia* 'La Paloma'
7. *Cryptanthus fosterianus*
8. *Begonia* 'Granada'
9. *Begonia* 'Dewdrop'

6-11 Walled Courtyard: Against what might be a stucco wall, a garden featuring exquisite leaf shapes and colors

MAGRITTE'S GARDEN

In his painting *Carte blanche*, the Belgian surrealist Rene Magritte (1898–1967) invents a kaleidoscopically fragmented world. We see a woman on horseback riding through a forest. The trees dissect the image, and several sections of the horse and rider have been replaced by distant forest. It's a thoroughly convincing but disquieting world, rendered with the precision of close observation on the one hand, and yet totally illogical on the other—it's perfectly surreal.

The interior landscape in figure 6-12 was completed before we gave it a name. Had we thought of the name earlier, we could have pursued the association with Magritte's painting much further. Plants, fake or real, could be pruned and positioned behind and in front of the

boards to create a three-dimensional version of his kind of illusion: irrational discontinuity that confuses foreground with background and positive space with negative space.

But it seems to us that the piece as constructed here already has a

certain ethereal, if not surreal, aspect: white on white, white boards against a white background, maybe calling to mind an aspen forest in winter. Would modifying the setup as suggested by figure 10-5 heighten the surreal aspect? No doubt it

would, but maybe at the cost of making it more kitschy. However, it's probably worth a try.

We used our fake figs yet again. But the real thing (*Ficus benjamina* cultivars) could have been used instead, even if we had further pursued the analogy with Magritte's painting.

Plants in figure 6-12:
1. fake fig (2 left and right)
2. *Rhipsalis paradoxa* (2 shocks)
3. *Begonia* 'Granada'
4. *Begonia* 'Kismet' (lower right)
5. *Brassaia arboricola* 'Dwarf'
6. *Begonia* 'Guy Savard'
7. *Paphiopedilum barbigerum*, smallest known paph
8. *Paphiopedilum sukhakulii*
9. *Brassaia arboricola* 'Variegated Dwarf'

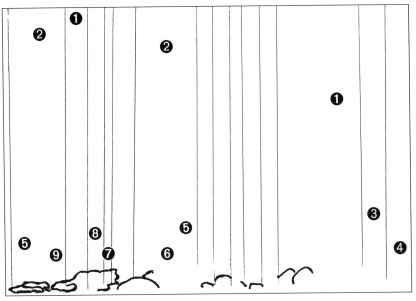

Diagram for 6-12

6-12 Magritte's Garden: A white-on-white confusion of positive and negative space, a device that might have amused Magritte

SEASONS IN THE GARDEN

Some poor souls live in climates with seasons but hate this one or that: They detest the plague of pollen in spring and fall, the cursed cold of winter, or the infernal heat of summer. But even these malcontents never say that they are bored with the seasons. They admit that each season stamps the landscape with its own brand of beauty—beauty that cannot be found in the sameness of the tropics and that must be acknowledged in spite of the sneezing, shivering, or sweating.

Inhabitants of temperate regions notice the year's passing. In fact, the seasons are a constant reminder of the passage of time and of one's mortality. Many of the seasonal effects we love are so fleeting, so elusive, that we never see enough of them to satisfy us, especially those of us in urban environments and without ready access to outdoor gardens. Often we wish that we could pull the seasons closer to us, and make them stay a little longer. That wish sometimes leads to a design with a seasonal theme.

That was our aim in setting up these variations (figures 6-13–6-15).

We were interested in a landscape that would reflect the seasons. But interiors where people live and work do not provide the kind of climate that favors plants of temperate regions—plants that require seasonal changes and respond to those changes in ways that characterize the seasons. The only way to get some of these effects indoors is to use preserved or artificial plant material, to refurbish the setup with plants of the season, or to use tropical plants that look as though they are seasonal.

What we decided to do here is use an infrastructure that implies a garden setting but not a time of year. The infrastructure could then be refitted as desired with different seasonal themes. In figure 6-14 the piece is outfitted as an autumn scene—dried grasses, bamboo, and painted pearwood branches suggest the season. Figure 6-15 shows the infrastructure devoid of plants and refitted with painted, shaped pieces of cottonwood. This setup alludes to winter, but perhaps not strongly enough to be convincing. Nevertheless, we think the design is strong enough in this bare-bones state to be of interest. In figure 6-13 the setup is furnished with plants, suggesting spring or summer. The plants used are from the tropics—they are grown for their foliage and have the same appearance yearlong.

Plants in figure 6-13:

1. *Rhipsalis capilliformis* (3 shocks, 1 lower)
2. *Tillandsia ionanthe* (2 clumps)
3. *Tillandsia usneoides* Spanish moss (several shocks)
4. *Rhipsalis paradoxa*
5. *Codonanthe crassifolia* (upper right)
6. *Brassaia arboricola* 'Dwarf' (several, 1 left)
7. *Brassaia arboricola* 'Variegated Dwarf' (2)
8. *Microsorum punctatum* 'Cristatum Dwarf'
9. *Calathea makoyana* peacock plant, a dwarf compact clone
10. *Rhipsalis teres*

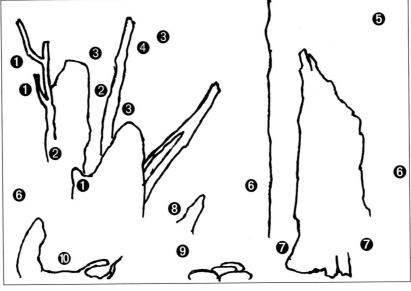

Diagram for 6-13

6-13 Seasons in the Garden (variation)

6-14 Seasons in the Garden

6-15 Seasons in the Garden (variation)

CHAPTER SEVEN

SEASONS

*L*iving in the tropics has its advantages, but the gift of four seasons is reserved only for those living in temperate regions. Only there does one get to enjoy that glorious four-act play of endless variety and change. There are always surprises, and no two performances are alike. Monotony is not a possibility, and every new season refreshes our senses and is cause for celebration. That's what we want to do in this chapter—celebrate the seasons with a few landscape designs.

Although there are no summer arrangements in this chapter, plant material available in that season can be used to refurbish fall and spring arrangements. Exactly what visual elements characterize summer is difficult to say, but if summer is thought to be the only season in the tropics, then most of our arrangements in chapters 1 and 3 can be seen as summer pieces.

Some of the pieces for spring and fall are not fixed in their effect but rather designed to incorporate an element of change and renewal. Each piece has two types of components, one permanent and the other temporary. The basic layout is permanent. But playing against the infrastructure are elements that must be replaced from time to time.

For example, a flowering branch of dogwood might play a key role in a spring arrangement, but its effect is short-lived and soon it becomes a sorry mess. You then have the freedom to refurbish the design with something fresh and at the height of its beauty. The same strategy works for several autumn pieces. Some fruit-bearing stems, seedpods, and grass plumes must be replaced with fresh material. Other infrastructures are neutral in their seasonal allusions and can be outfitted quite differently depending on the time of year and availability of materials. While some people will view refurbishing a setup as a chore, others will see it as an opportunity to inject a bit of their own taste and personality into the piece.

Of course, instead of using materials harvested from real plants, we could use artificial substitutes. The best of these fakes are so well made that they are nearly indistinguishable from the real thing even when the two are placed side by side. However, all the plant materials in the pieces shown in this chapter are real.

Most of our fall scenes and all of our winter scenes are composed entirely of permanent materials and do not need to be refreshed at all. The winter scenes in particular so strongly suggest their season that no easy modification will convincingly represent another season. But the static quality of the winter landscape is part of its essence. And including transitory elements would not honor the look of this season—spare, seemingly lifeless, pure in form and color. Such elements would lessen the drama, and it's the drama of winter that moves us most of all (figure 7-1).

7-1 **Forever winter at the foot of Franz Josef Glacier, South Island, New Zealand**

WINDOW ON THE SEASONS

Seasonal change is the great gift that nature bestows on the temperate regions, and we planned our own outdoor garden so that it would make the most of this gift. We designed the garden to be interesting in a distinctively different way in each season, and we made certain that every window in the house framed a view of the garden: a rock arrangement from this window, a planting of spring bulbs from that, ornamental grasses from another. But our favorite views are from the windows that have a tree planted nearby—a flowering tree, a fruiting tree, or a tree that is spectacular in fall color. These trees are planted far enough away and pruned thinly enough so that only a branch or two crosses the window—perfect to herald the seasons but not obstruct the larger view of the garden. The effect is spare, but you don't walk by the window without noticing it.

The window frame and the view to the outside led to the piece in figure 7-2. Here the abstracted window frame provides a structure to hang plants on, a frame for the arrangement, and an object that has some design interest of its own. This frame is made out of wood, but all sorts of other materials are suitable. We chose fruiting stems of a cotoneaster (*Cotoneaster horizontalis*) to furnish the frame—the fruit is very long-lasting and holds its color well. However, all sorts of other fruiting branches (fake or real) could be used. The frame could be refurbished according to the seasons: evergreen branches in the winter, flowering branches in the spring or summer, branches with colorful leaves in autumn. Of course, the contrarian could ignore seasonal availability of real plant material and furnish the frame with artificial plants characteristic of a different season.

7-2 Window on the Seasons: Autumn

WINTER SOLSTICE

The most dramatic season is winter. Gone are the flowery frills of spring and the flamboyant trappings of autumn. Snow and ice pare down the landscape to its essential core. The bare-bones structure of rocks and trees is now clear to the eye— no unctuous bowing of grass, no fluttering of leaves—all needless motion is suspended. Life on the edge, frozen to a standstill. The cold even squeezes out color, leaving nothing but a symphony of silvery gray, black, and white.

There is a crispness to these tones that makes them crackle in high contrast, hard and brittle. And the lack of color modulation seems to alter the geometry of space itself— successive planes appear com-

pressed, as though seen through a telephoto lens. This also adds to the drama. Here is the landscape distilled to its essence, with nothing left to distract us from its fundamental form (figure 7-3). This is the mood we attempted to evoke in the piece shown in figure 7-4 as well as in the

following winter pieces—cold and austere, uncompromisingly direct and simple.

The piece in figure 7-4 can be seen as a frozen cascade, the black boulders of its river not yet covered by snow or ice. Or we may see it as a switchback on a mountain trail

leading through a rockfall along successive ridges to higher ground. Or maybe the piece shows staggered snowbanks compressed against each other by the lack of color and flat lighting of a cloudy winter day. In each of these interpretations, the black-lacquered branches suggest the tracery of a deciduated forest. On the other hand, maybe the piece is abstract enough to resist any of these interpretations.

The black vertical slats and blue-gray horizontal walls were built out of boards purchased at a lumber-yard. The boards were cut, painted, and then assembled. The stones are ordinary fieldstones painted black. The black "trees" are painted branches cut from a honey locust.

7-3 On the winter route to Dream Lake, Rocky Mountain National Park, Colorado

7-4 Winter Solstice

AUTUMN RUINS

Buildings also have their seasons: a spring of construction, a summer of usefulness, an autumn of disrepair and collapse, and finally a bulldozer burial beginning an endless winter. But even a building in decline can be fascinating long after its architectural interest has vanished. Some of the fascination may rest on seeing the life of the building as a metaphor for human life. Or it may be pure nostalgia, remembering our lives when the building was young. But some of the fascination may come from viewing the remains of the building as part of the landscape, now complementing it rather than dominating it.

Our appreciation of these landscapes is also seasonal. We like them best in late autumn, when the leaves are off the trees and the snow has not yet obscured the ruins. Blocks of stone and concrete are now exposed, and grasses provide contrast. Freeform natural elements set against the harsh geometry of manufactured elements is always a formula that captures our attention.

The piece in figure 7-5 plays off of this theme —twigs and dried grasses are arranged around blocks of concrete. The color is low-key, very much in the spirit of late autumn. Although we have tried to make the contrast between the various components of the design as strong as possible, we still see this piece as a landscape. But those who think we have gone too far in the direction of abstraction may argue that the arrangement makes no reference to landscapes whatsoever.

7-5　Autumn Ruins

FIRST SNOW

Perhaps figure 7-6 is a portrait of late autumn or early winter. There has been a dusting of snow —enough to cover the ground with a white sheet but not enough to flatten the grasses or cling to the branches. In morning or evening light, snow has a silvery blue-gray hue, very much like the color of the lighter boards.

Perhaps this is the edge of a forest of trees with trunks so dark they appear black in this light. The dark horizontal bands could represent fallen branches or maybe bands of rock partly hidden under snow-covered turf. Red-twig dogwood (*Cornus sericea*) lends a bit of color to the scene—color that is at its best during the dormant season. Strange that it presents its liveliest color during the season in which it seems least alive! The only other color in this piece is the subtle auburn tones of the sprigs of bamboo.

Besides paring it down to a more austere version composed of nothing but the black-and-gray panel structure, how else might we have handled this setup? We could have used nothing but colonies of white branches, say of a fastigiate pear tree (see figures 7-10 and 7-11) or maybe a few white branches with a strong horizontal line to suggest wide-spreading trees. Or we could have reworked the design without using branches at all but rather various grasses. Another option would be to rework it without any plant material (except for the boards and panels of the infrastructure) and use black- or white-painted stone. There are many possibilities, some closer to pure abstraction, others to the more accepted notions of landscape.

7-6 First Snow: Only a few remnants of autumn survive

EXIT AUTUMN

This is not high autumn, with its binge of incendiary color. Rather, this is autumn at the edge of winter, when there is still some color, but it is dispersed and muted. Some grasses still stand in defiance of the coming season, but not for long. Winter is in the air; soon the landscape will be repainted in black and white, and even this little bit of color will be a memory. It's a landscape poised in anticipation of a great change. It is the moods of this moment of the year that we have tried to hint at in this piece (figure 7-7).

Some may see the piece as being too small to be thought of as a landscape. They may see it as more of an arrangement, something closer to ikebana in spirit. We think the piece does not suggest great size: The grasses alone limit the height. Of course, one could rework the piece using much larger blocks of stone and pieces of wood, as well as larger grasses and bamboo, such as dried corn stalks and giant reed grass (*Arundo donax*). Still, the height would be limited to a mere 15 ft (4.5 m) or so—but maybe that would be large enough. However, one can imagine an even larger interpretation where branches of trees and shrubs replace the grasses, perhaps like the treatment seen in figure 7-11.

But even in a larger realization, the piece in figure 7-7 would have a self-contained aspect rather than appearing to be a fragment of a larger scene. We have seen such isolated arrangements of stone, wood, and grasses composed by nature in a barren field, or on the banks of a river, or against a canyon wall. So without apology, we declare this to be a landscape.

Here we used only grasses: *Panicum virgatum* 'Heavy Metal' at the top; *Chasmanthium latifolium*, northern sea oats, left; *Arundinaria viridistriata*, a hardy bamboo, right. But fields and gardens have all sorts of other materials that would be just as suitable. And you can always go to a local craft shop and get the latest in dried weeds.

7-7 **Exit Autumn**

THE COLORS OF AUTUMN

In this piece (figure 7-8), roots and branches are arranged on blocks of concrete. Dried grasses and leaves of bamboo reflect autumn's more conservative side, while branches of red-twig dogwood (*Cornus sericea*) bring more assertive color to the arrangement. But the most striking bit of color is supplied by three star-shaped bromeliads on the wood. From top to bottom, these cryptanthus hybrids are: 'Rubra,' 'Pink Starlit,' and 'It.' Of course, their inclusion here is a bit of a deceit. Their color is certainly that of autumn, but in their tropical home they never experience the meaning of the season. They would turn up their roots and die if a frost accosted them. Yet frost temperatures are exactly what is needed to trigger the change from the tired greens of late summer to the vibrant warm colors of autumn. Unfortunately, the plants of temperate regions usually object to indoor conditions, and their fall color is transitory. But for our "earth stars" it's always autumn — at least as far as color goes — and they grow quite happily under normal room conditions.

Hundreds of other bromeliads boast autumn finery all year. You can choose between solid colors in red, yellow, burgundy, copper, orange, and silver; between shapes that compare to stars, urns, tubes, and fountains; between patterns in longitudinal stripes, transverse stripes, spots, dots, chevrons, and hieroglyphics. Most are easy to grow and many are readily available. Other plants, such as Rex begonias, could be used for a touch of autumn color, but none are as dependable as the bromeliads, particularly the cryptanthus.

7-8 **The Colors of Autumn: Reflected in tropical plants that know no seasons**

A WINTER FOG

Sometimes the cold of a winter's night wrings the slightest bit of moisture out of the air, and morning sees the moisture suspended as a low-hanging blanket of fog. The taller trees rise above it and seem to hover there, free of gravity and any attachment to the earth. It's an effect that can occur in any season, but it is most magical and exciting in winter.

In an attempt to capture this, we constructed a geometric abstraction in black, gray, and white (figure 7-9). To an asymmetric wooden lattice we attached horizontal members representing a succession of ridges in the landscape. Rows of honeylocust branches painted black were secured to the lattice at various heights above the floor to suggest that their bases were concealed by fog.

7-9 Trees suspended in A Winter Fog

WINTER RAVINE

It's one thing to see the canyon in spring, summer, or fall, but quite something else to see it in winter. In the warmer seasons you hike along the canyon rim and peer into the gorge, down to the ribbon of water far below. The canyon is too steep to descend, and the water too turbulent to wade across. So you see only the opposite wall of the canyon, and only from one side.

But in the winter, when icy temperatures have taken hold and the river has frozen deeply enough, you can walk through the ravine on this trail of ice. Now the walls of the canyon rise high above you on both sides, and at their bases the vast vertical folds of rock conform to the serpentine course of the river. Some parts of the wall, where the low winter sun has access, show the black color of the bare stone; other parts are nearly white with snow and ice. Occasionally a small stand of trees or a group of shrubs, dormant for the season, etch their bare linear structure against the canyon.

Many canyons fit this description, but we were recalling our favorite—Glacier Gorge in Rocky Mountain National Park, Colorado— while we worked on this setup (figure 7-10). Hoping to hint at the stark grandeur of this ravine in winter, we wanted the piece to suggest great size. We have no difficulty imagining the branches as trees 20 or 30 ft (6 or 9 m) tall, and the entire construction as 40 ft (12 m) from floor to ceiling.

The three pale gray panels are from our Capitol Reef background, and the black panels are merely painted boards 1 in (2.5 cm) thick and of varying length. The "trees," painted black or white, are cuttings from a fastigiate variety of pear tree—the narrow, upright branching pattern being better than a wide-spreading pattern in suggesting height. The red branches are unpainted cuttings taken from a little-leaf linden. A cluster of dried weeds, purchased at a craft store, is placed in the foreground to complete the arrangement.

In a realization that is large enough, the panels could define corridors for people to walk through. The corridors, out of view to those standing in front of the construction, could continue the pattern of gray and black paneling, and groups of trees could be placed along the walls. This is definitely not the warmest and most inviting piece that we have designed, but that in part is the point of it.

7-10 Winter Ravine

FIRE AND ICE

7-11 Fire and Ice: A bit of warm color in the cold of winter

Nothing injects more excitement into the winter landscape than a few strokes of color. A bit of red, in particular, will grab your attention and rivet your gaze—the hottest color against the coldest landscape—fire and ice.

Such a combination is not that common, at least not where we live. But a few shrubs and even some trees have red stems throughout winter. Red-twig dogwood (*Cornus sericea*), especially young stems less than two years old, give the effect as reliably as anything else (figure 7-11). They positively glow when lit from behind. However, the effect is not permanent. After a few weeks, the color becomes muted and later completely corrupts to a nondescript brown-black. We restored their color by painting them.

The white branches were cut from a particularly fastigiate variety of pear tree and then painted. We used panels from two different sets—our Canyonlands and Maligne Canyon set—to form the background. The cobbles were found in a nearby field and then painted black. The wood is from a fallen cottonwood tree.

FOUR SEASONS

Springtime in the Rockies is renowned in poetry and song. But in truth it is only a "sometimes" season: Sometimes it lasts for a glorious three months, sometimes it's cancelled altogether. Winter might take a day or two off, giving us sunshine and 60° F (12.2° C) weather—leaves appear, things begin to sprout, buds swell and open. Then winter returns and ices the awakening. In the Rockies, spring is precious, and we enjoy it when we can, indoors as well as outdoors. When branches of forsythia, flowering quince, or crabapple come into bud, we harvest them for indoor display. Usually we stick them in a vase without much thought or ceremony. But our enjoyment is much greater when we take the time to arrange them in a setting specially designed to receive such gifts. That is the purpose of the piece in figure 7-12: to receive such gifts. Without them, the piece is rather bland. But throughout spring and summer we have a steady supply of flowering branches to refurbish it again and again.

Autumn and winter require different treatments. Colored branches, branches with leaves in fall color or in fruit, or branches with fall flowers can be used. Evergreen boughs are available in a number of colors and patterns throughout the year. Add to this seedpods and dried grasses, and this piece can be used as a foil for arrangements year-round. However, the piece does need some maintenance, not only in changing the display, but also in tidying up the arrangement occasionally: Fallen fruit, spent blossoms, and dried leaves must be removed. Of course, the use of seasonal artificial materials is another solution.

In this midspring version we used only real plants. At the top are flowering branches of the dwarf sour cherry North Star (*Prunus cerasus* 'North Star'); the red flowers are those of the eastern flowering dogwood Cherokee Chief (*Cornus florida* 'Cherokee Chief'). Growing well in its pot at the bottom of the arrangement and looking like it was hammered out of a sheet of silver is the begonia 'Kismet.' Whereas the flowering branches were presentable for a mere forty-eight hours, the begonia is a permanent feature. However, cleanup of the branches was easy, and refurbishing the piece presented no problem.

This piece works throughout the year, but it is the spring show that gives us the most pleasure.

7-12 Four Seasons: A piece designed to host any season, shown here furnished with a spring theme

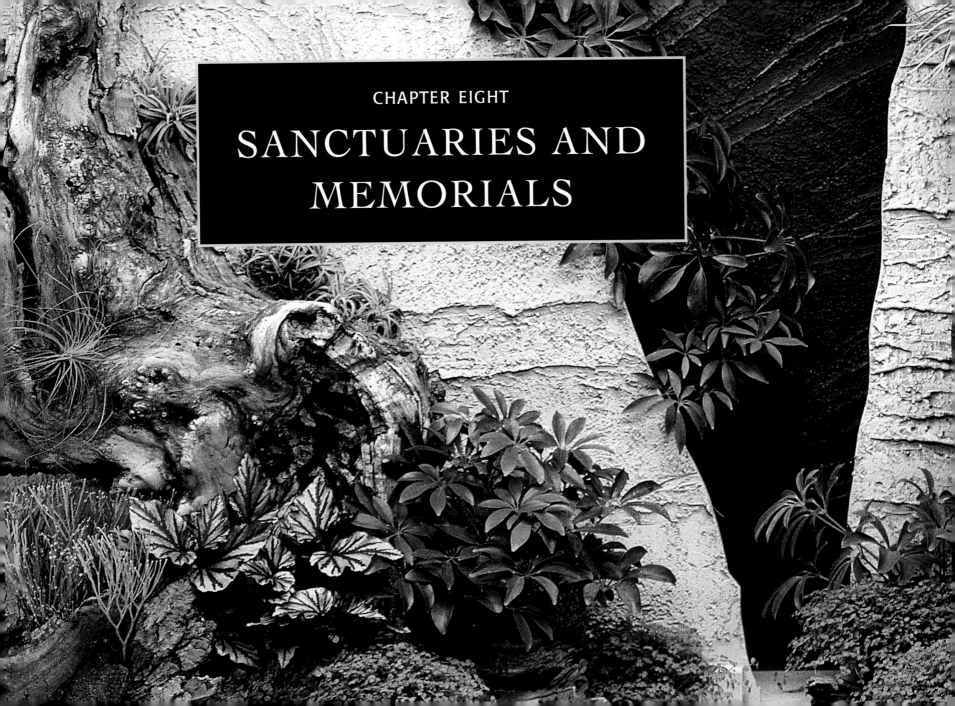

CHAPTER EIGHT

SANCTUARIES AND MEMORIALS

So often have we found solace and renewed optimism in the solitude of a wilderness landscape that we have to wonder whether it is mere conditioning or some inherent response common to all of us. So many people react in the same way to the landscape that we have come to believe the latter. We think that there are visual aspects of wilderness landscapes that affect us all in the same way, causing us to reflect or calming us and lifting our spirits. Likewise, designed landscapes can elicit similar responses to some degree. Hoping to do just that, we created the pieces in this chapter.

These are quiet pieces, pieces designed for meditation. They are meant to encourage introspection and communicate a sense of solitude while inviting the viewer to take an imaginary journey through the landscape. Visually these landscapes are spare, and in some cases even austere—any appearance of clutter would work counter to our purpose. Most of the designs use a minimum of color, and even then the color is subdued. In some cases, a receding succession of panels is used to imply depth and lend a sense of mystery to the scene. Living plants, when they are used, are used sparingly. If a season is suggested, it is usually winter. If a time of day is suggested, it is late evening or early morning. While these pieces certainly are not ebullient, we do not think of them as being in any way dour. We instead see them as low-key and controlled.

The uncompromising directness and simplicity of most of these designs offer few cues as to size. The pieces are in this sense scale-independent: Any realization from a few feet to a few stories tall will work. But usually a larger setup is more effective than a smaller one.

Bare branches are frequently used in the arrangements to suggest trees. Some may see them as dead trees, an allusion to our own mortality. Others may interpret them as dormant trees with all the promise of a spring awakening. We sometimes had these interpretations in mind, but neither played a crucial role in designing the pieces, and neither need play a role in evaluating their effectiveness. The branches provided a linear element while emphasizing the spare quality of the designs. Seeing them as trees reinforces the view that these settings are indeed landscapes.

In a large-scale version of these designs one could use real trees, perhaps stabilized by a coating of epoxy, urethane, or polyester. Since they can be painted any color, the form of the trees is the most important consideration. Alternatively, one could construct artificial trees through a variety of methods (see page 17). Similarly, stones and boulders of some size also can be constructed out of lightweight artificial materials (see page 18).

All of these pieces need room. They must be isolated from distractions in order to communicate a sense of solitude and tranquility. Aside from this, there are no other restrictions on placement.

RENEWAL

Walk through a great forest and you see the signs of renewal everywhere: young growth maturing, aging, dying, and returning to the soil, and then from that enriched soil, new growth beginning again. A single tree may take decades or even generations to mature. Then, weakened by old age, a storm may take it down in seconds, scattering broken branches all about, and leaving nothing standing except giant snags of its trunk. Its well-decayed heartwood will prepare the soil to receive the seeds of a new generation. And within a season or a year, vibrant young plants will take hold.

We attempted to capture the contrast between new growth and old growth in this piece, and to hint at the process of renewal. Figure 8-1 shows the piece without plants, and figure 8-2 shows the piece with plants. The first version may be taken as a landscape in its own right, alluding to the time shortly after the tree's fall and before new growth has begun. This bare version may

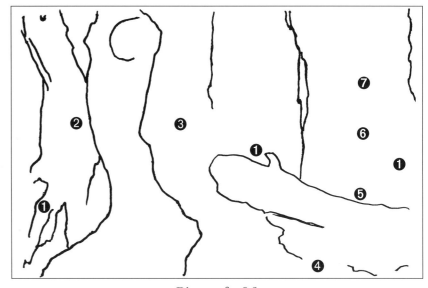

Diagram for 8-2

8-1 Renewal: Dead trees become nurseries for new plants

have more impact initially. But the second, which has more elements and is more complicated, perhaps sustains interest longer.

Plants in figure 8-2:
1. *Microsorum punctatum* 'Cristatum Dwarf' (also mid-right and far right)
2. *Miltonidium* Pupukea 'Sunset'
3. *Aspidistra elatior* 'Milky Way' cast-iron plant
4. *Cryptanthus* 'Pink Starlit' (bottom)

5. *Rodriguezia secunda*, small orchid with a many-flowered stem of orange flowers
6. *Paphiopedilum Maudiae* 'Magnificum,' renowned slipper orchid, here with two blossoms striped white and green
7. *Paphiopedilum* Larry Bird, a broken stem of this superb multiflowered slipper orchid, unceremoniously slam-dunked into a hole in the wood, where it will last in good condition for weeks

8-2 Renewal: The old gives rise to the new

ROCKFALL ELEGY

We wanted an imposing piece that gave no clue to its exact size but suggested something monumental, even at the cost of it being impersonal. Something that would have a strong, distinctive presence and yet would complement an architectural setting. This (figures 8-3 and 8-4) is what we came up with. As abstract as this piece is, we see it as a landscape. The mood is intentionally somber; the color scheme, gray and black. The elemental forms are meant to convey a sense of strength and permanence.

The piece was assembled out of precast concrete blocks (cinderblocks) and painted stone. In a large version, the concrete blocks would be hollow. The stones also would be hollow, sculpted in epoxy, cast in metal, or fabricated out of concrete (see page 18). The background, modeled after what is called pagoda rock, plays an important role as a textural and tonal component of the design.

What happens when you add plants to this composition? Is the overall effect enhanced or diminished? Does the added contrast in color and form give the piece more interest, or is it merely distracting? With the exception of the epiphytic cactus, we chose desert plants rather

Diagram for 8-4

than jungle tropicals to furnish the piece. The colors of many desert plants tend toward grays and blues, colors much more likely to complement the rock and concrete than the more strident greens of jungle plants. In form, most desert plants are nearly abstract, and thus closer to the spirit of the infrastructure. The gentler flowing lines of tropical foliage would blunt the hardedge geometry of the stone and concrete and soften the piece, robbing it of much of its strength. Undoubtedly, some will prefer the planted version. But we prefer the simpler variation without plants.

Plants in figure 8-4:
1. *Seyrigia humbertii*
2. *Ceropegia woodii*, rosary vine (2 shocks cascading down the cinderblocks), hardy drought-tolerant succulent vine with freely produced, wondrously strange flowers
3. *Euphorbia lactea* 'Cristata,' (2) widely adaptable, slow-growing to 6 ft (1.8 m)
4. *Senecio haworthii* (several, right)
5. *Echeveria* 'Alpine Rose' (3 on ground lower left), not potted, but will last for months, maybe indefinitely, if occasionally sprayed

8-3 Rockfall Elegy: a landscape bordering on pure abstraction

8-4 Rockfall Elegy: a few plants moderate the severity of the previous setup

FOR THOSE ABSENT

In recent years, yellow ribbons and yellow banners have come to symbolize grief and concern for absent loved ones. So we thought that introducing yellow fabric into the design of a memorial piece was appropriate. We designed two pieces using this device, both variations on a winter theme, both using the fabric to suggest water in motion.

The first piece (figure 8-6) can be seen as a view through a narrow canyon. In the distance, a waterfall drops from the canyon's rim into a river hidden from view. The illusion of depth and the unseen crash of the waterfall on the rocks below impart a sense of mystery to the scene. The tree branches, taken from a pear tree, are placed to suggest a stand of trees growing at the entrance to the canyon. Several bunches of dried flowers play the role of dormant shrubs in the understory. It's winter in the canyon, morning or evening, and everything is leafless and dry. But water is flowing, and spring will come.

8-5 Double waterfall and black lake on the island of Kauai, Hawaii

8-6 For Those Absent: A canyon waterfall

FOR THOSE ABSENT II

Here again (figure 8-8) yellow banners suggest moving water. This, too, is a canyon scene. In this version, the waterfall is split into two parts, and we can see the water crashing onto the boulders at the bottom of the canyon and then roiling away downstream. But in spite of all the implied turbulence, the piece communicates a sense of calm and permanence—even the banners do not seem out of character with the controlled nature of the design. This may be due to the simplicity of forms and the uncluttered arrangement. Or, perhaps, to the colors—dark and somber in spite of the high-key yellow banners. Again, the split wall contributes to the illusion of depth. A tree growing in isolation is precariously perched on a ledge near the edge of the water. The tree is dormant, awaiting the arrival of spring.

8-7 A waterfall tumbles down the black cliffs of the ravine carved out by the Franz Josef Glacier, South Island, New Zealand

8-8 For Those Absent II: Again, a waterfall set deep in a canyon

WINTER STORM

Sometimes nature's mood seems to resonate with our own. And when sadness is the mood, sensing that resonance is comforting. It's as though we are sharing our deepest emotions with a force larger than ourselves, a force outside ourselves. And this gives us a new perspective. Externalizing grief helps us to cope with it.

Monuments and sanctuaries respect these deep emotions by reflecting them. They do not trivialize them by offering a pretty distraction—that would not assuage grief, it would exacerbate it. We want the piece to echo our state of mind and communicate a sense of empathy directly and sincerely, without calling great attention to itself.

Here (figures 8-9 and 8-10) we have chosen two close variations on a winter theme: a grove of deciduated trees at the entrance to a canyon. The dark walls of the canyon are in stark contrast to the white trees. The entire piece suggests an impending storm. Foreboding, but we know that it will pass.

The trees here are pear wood branches, chosen for their fastigiate growth habit. The bark, naturally a pale gray, was darker than we wanted, and so we painted them. The panels used as the background in figure 8-9 were rearranged to form the canyon of the piece in figure 8-10: The right and left panels were rotated 180 degrees and interchanged. In either setup, the white floor can be viewed as ice.

Again, the designs do not dictate scale. We can see either of them staged in a 6-ft- (1.8-m-) wide recess in a wall, or against a wall 30 ft (9 m) wide. Of course, the larger realization would be more effective, and at such a size the piece could be designed so that visitors could walk into the canyon and explore the side paths. Benches could be placed within the piece to allow visitors to sit in solitude.

8-9 Winter Storm

8-10 Winter Storm (variation)

CANYONS

We have seen great canyons where lesser canyons meet, and where their streams converge into a great river. If you stand at the mouth of one of these canyons and look upstream, you see the walls of the side canyons as a succession of planes receding into the distance. Only a bend in the river prevents you from seeing further.

If we could walk into the canyon and explore the river, what would we find? what would we learn? But we don't dare enter—the danger of a sudden surge of water, a flash flood, keeps us out. The walls are so steep and slippery that they offer no escape. So we stand at the canyon's mouth and look into it as far as we can, wondering what is behind the bend.

In designing the piece in figures 8-11 and 8-12 we wanted to suggest the geometry of such a canyon and

the mood that it evokes. A staggered series of panels plays the role of the side canyons, some in shadow, some not. Parts of trees appear to have been washed downstream and have become lodged at various points at the base of the canyon. In the planted version, the plants might be seen

as living trees and shrubs that have taken hold on the canyon walls or on the narrow banks of the river.

Which version do we prefer? Certainly, the first is more imposing. But the second is more approachable. The choice depends on the setting, the intended purpose of the

piece, and the desires of those who will see it.

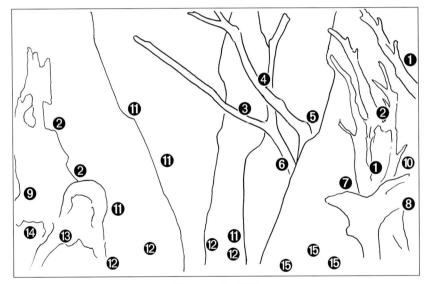

Diagram for 8-12

Plants in figure 8-12:
1. *Tillandsia argentea* (2 in flower far right)
2. *Tillandsia ionantha,* (3 clusters, right and left)
3. *Tillandsia abidida*
4. *Tillandsia butzii*
5. *Tillandsia gemniflora*
6. *Tillandsia caput-medusae*
7. *Tillandsia streptophylla*
8. *Tillandsia usneoides* Spanish moss
9. *Tillandsia filifolia*
10. *Neoregelia tigrina*
11. *Brassaia arboricola* (several)
12. *Ficus pumila* 'Quercifolia' (4)
13. *Begonia* 'Kismet'
14. *Psilotum nudum*
15. fake moss (several on bare floor)

8-11 Canyons: A convergence

8-12 Canyons (with plants)

PASSAGE

Even in the city, where land comes at a corporate price and is valued for its vertical potential as well as for its surface area, a place of worship often has a garden. It might not be a large garden, but it is a space where you can stroll in the open air, be alone with your thoughts, and leave the physical and spiritual confines of the building behind.

If the building is large, old, and grand, the passage from the building's interior to the garden outside may lead through a massive set of doors and down a flight of oversized stairs. But regardless of the building's scale or age, the passage should be special. After all, it's a bridge between two worlds—two distinctly different, reverent expressions of the human spirit.

This is what we had in mind when we designed the piece in figures 8-13 and 8-14, although there are several different ways to interpret it. We can imagine it to be the entrance to a passageway that leads from the interior of a place of worship out into a garden. The path is not direct; a couple of turns are needed to get you there.

The walls of the corridor continue the visual theme of the piece: stucco colored and textured, as in the center panels; or one wall treated this way and the opposite wall painted black; or each wall made of alternating panels of gray stucco and black.

The visual theme continues into the garden itself, in which the walls are also faced with stucco to match the center panels of the piece. Potted plants placed in the corridor near the entrance to the garden further moderate the transition from interior to exterior. The branch that is part of the piece has a living counterpart outside in the garden: a tree or large shrub growing near the entrance. We imagine the garden to be neither formal nor abstract, and certainly not ostentatious.

But there are other possible interpretations of this piece. It can be a screen in back of the pulpit. The panels of the screen can conceal cabinets where scrolls, robes, or furnishings required by the service are stored.

The piece has a modular aspect to it that suggests it could be joined side by side with variations to form a wall. Extended in this way, it could be the wall behind the choir, textured and configured to be acoustically correct. Maybe for this application the version without plants (figure 8-13) is more appropriate.

In a secular or nonsecular setting, with walking space between the panels, shelves can be affixed to either side of the panels to create a library wall. Freestanding versions can allow for more shelving away from the walls.

Even with all of these various possibilities in mind, we find the first one the most exciting.

Plants in figure 8-14:
1. *Rhipsalis paradoxa*
2. *Tillandsia ionantha* (3 clusters)
3. *Hatiora salicornioides* (4 shocks)
4. *Ficus pumila* (3)
5. *Gypsophila paniculata*, dried and dyed white
6. *Polyscias fruticosa* 'Dwarf' (2 groups)
7. fake moss (several on floor)

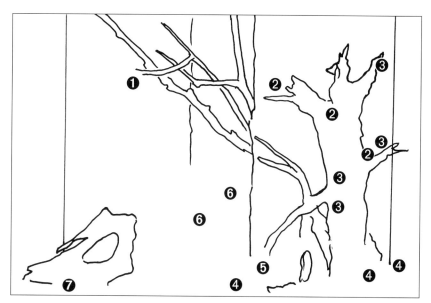

Diagram for 8-14

8-13 Passage: Perhaps through a canyon

8-14 Passage (with plants)

FRAGRANCE

Among the many orchids renowned for their fragrance, none are more famous than the angraecoids. Most are native to Africa and Madagascar, but there are a few representatives in the United States, including the ghost orchid (*Polyradacion lindenii*), the target of the orchid thief in the book by the same name.

The serenely beautiful white flowers of the angraecoids and their intense evening fragrance lure moths that pollinate them. One of the most spectacular, the Star of Africa, has a 12-in (30-cm) nectar tube that hangs from the back of its lip.

We find the angraecoids with their exquisite blossoms and their intoxicating fragrance irresistible, and several different kinds have found their way into our collection. A couple can be seen in figure 4-4, but our favorite is the one pictured here, *Angraecum* Longiscott. As though the pristine, crystalline beauty and intense, heady fragrance of the 4-in (10-cm) blossoms were not enough, the plant offers them perfectly arranged in two rows on a raceme holding up to twenty at a time. The 10-in (25-cm) nectaries form a loose curtain of thick white threads that hang against a fan of dark green leaves. A mature plant may produce two or three spikes at a time and the flowers last for six weeks or more. But even when the plant is not in bloom, its two-dimensional, opposite-alternate leaf pattern makes a strong design contribution.

It is easy but essential to meet the cultural requirements of this exquisite plant. Light demands are moderate; high humidity is required. Of course, one could substitute with plants with even fewer demands and a much longer blooming period—moth orchids (phalaenopsis), for example. But none can match the combined beauty and fragrance of Longiscott.

In this arrangement you see Longiscott displayed against our pale gray Capitol Reef wall. The contrast between the wall and the blossoms is minimal, which gives the piece an ethereal quality. Conversely, the sharp contrast between the wall and the dark wood and green foliage gives the design some tension. Although the background of this setup is the same as that in figures 5-3 and 6-9, its more controlled design and restricted space make it better suited as a sanctuary piece.

Plants in figure 8-15, clockwise from left:
Begonia 'Brown Swirl'
Angraecum Longiscott (5)
Microsorum punctatum 'Cristatum Dwarf'
fake moss (many)

8-15 Fragrance: These orchids will scent an entire room

CHAPTER NINE

NEITHER HERE NOR THERE

*T*his is a catchall collection of pieces that fit neither here nor there in the earlier chapters. Some pieces came about from multiple influences converging into a single plan—perhaps an idea for texture from one source, composition from another, and color from a third. The goal then became to make a coherent whole that was greater than the sum of its parts.

Sometimes, in the course of developing an idea, the design changed as certain features became unworkable, either for practical reasons or because of design limitations, and we saw that we could continue in some other direction. Several such turns occasionally led to something worthwhile and occasionally to something completely disappointing. The acceptable designs often showed their varied origins. But rather than resulting in a muddle of disparate themes, this gave the design an unexpected visual tension that increased its interest.

In some cases, when playing with materials, we stumbled upon a design idea that captured our attention. Curious to see where it would lead, we pursued it. Usually the path led to a dead-end, but once in a while we were pleasantly surprised.

Often we were trying to capture a certain mood or effect. To better understand what components were responsible for the effect and how they worked, we pushed the design toward abstraction, getting rid of what seemed irrelevant or superfluous. This reductive approach can be quite fruitful when it leads to a new piece—and quite exciting when the piece offers something new.

There were times when our interest was purely formal: Will this combination of colors work? What about this allocation of positive and negative masses? Is this an effective background? Again a rather analytical approach, but one that often proves fruitful.

Sometimes we even tried to inject a bit of humor into a piece, or come precariously close to the edge of crassness without falling over. There was little risk in this risk-taking and possibly something to be gained.

We have had great fun designing these neither-here-nor-there pieces. At least it was great fun when it worked. And when it worked, the outcome often left us feeling a bit like explorers in a new land.

TRI-X STRUT

Webster's College Dictionary defines strut as:

(1) To walk with a vain, pompous bearing. (2) Any of various structural members, as in trusses, primarily intended to resist longitudinal compression.

Perhaps it's a stretch, but one might see the Xs in this piece (figures 9-1 and 9-2) as three figures striding through the landscape. Their attitude does seem a bit arrogant, but vain and pompous? They have no structural purpose in this piece, but there is no reason why they could not be put to such use in a large-scale realization.

Here their primary function is visual. They are made of wood, but they could be plastic, metal, or any other material appropriate for the particular site. Their simple, bold geometry provides sharp contrast to the softer forms of the plants. And the abstract quality they lend to the design makes it scale-independent,

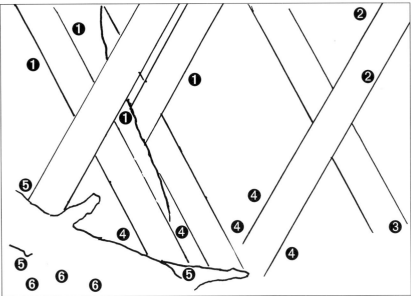

Diagram for 9-2

although an inherent monumentality argues for a very large realization, say two or three stories high. Of course, at such a size, a different set of plants would be needed. But there are so many to choose from that this would not be a problem.

This is another example where geometric components are set off against naturalistic ones to create the kind of visual tension we love to explore.

Plants in figure 9-2, clockwise from upper left:
1. *Ficus pumila* 'Variegata' (4)
2. *Chlorophytum comosum* 'Mandaianum'
3. *Syngonium* 'Dwarf' (several)
4. *Chlorophytum bichetii* (5)
5. *Selaginella kraussiana* 'Aurea' (many)
6. fake moss (many)

9-1 Tri-X Strut (detail)

9-2 Tri-X Strut

BI-X TANGO

It takes two to tango, and the two are usually dressed in black: macho black for the man; sultry, slinky black for the woman. They move as one, with a stilted syncopation that communicates a suave but keyed-up sexuality. It may be a bit over-the-top, but you have to admit it's a dance of high drama.

The title did not precede the design (figure 9-3)—after the piece was completed, the two tango dancers emerged and the title was inescapable. Why the tango? It was more than just the two black figures that prompted the title. The spirit of the dance itself seemed to have some expression in the piece: The opposing diagonals of the Xs suggested the syncopated rhythm, and their placement against the strong vertical and horizontal lines of the lattice added tension. The contrast between the flowing red banners and the dark colors of the backdrop seemed to capture some of the fire and passion of the dance. So Bi-X Tango it became.

9-3 Bi-X Tango

SOLO DANCER

Hot on the heels of our last couple is this solo dancer (figure 9-4). The stage has been reworked and now appears to be a garden. Evening is the time, and autumn is the season. A bit of mystery and drama anticipate the performance as the dancer enters from behind the screen. It's a striking figure that we see, taut and slender and clothed entirely in black.

How much of the design of this piece and the two preceding it was inspired by the interpretation? Not a bit! Their common compositional elements relate them. Here we have added several honeylocust branches painted white.

The mood evoked differs from piece to piece. Of course, our own mood inevitably enters into the design. That mood may change as the design progresses, and the direction of the piece might take a sudden turn as wrenching as a tango twist. But changes in these three pieces were brought about by design considerations. Programmatic interpretation was an afterthought.

9-4 Solo Dancer

WATCHERS

With this piece we explored one of our favorite themes: the interplay of industrial objects and natural objects. We like using the former in ways other than those intended by the manufacturer, and we like using the latter in any way whatsoever, particularly if most people would consider the objects to be worthless or useless. In figures 9-5 and 9-6, the commercial components are pressed-wood panels painted white, and the natural components are pieces of wood found lying in the nearby fields.

After arranging the panels and the pieces of wood, we stood back and took a look. For a moment, we saw the white boards as an aspen forest in winter, and the field wood as creatures staring out at us. They were watching us and we were watching them. That gave us what little we needed to come up with the title. With no further thought of a possible connection to its title, we went back to work on the piece and set up two versions.

In the first (figure 9-5) we used only one plant, the earth star *Cryptanthus fosterianus,* one of our favorite bromeliads. Each purple-brown leaf sports a column of silver chevrons —it's an eye-catcher wherever you place it but also a team player that won't steal the show. The piece has an icy, detached quality, even with this one plant; without it, it's too austere. In the second version (figure 9-6) we added more plants to soften the effect and make a warmer piece. Unfortunately, it was at the expense of the allusion to the watchers, and we much prefer the first version.

Plants in figure 9-6:
1. *Ceropegia woodii,* rosary vine (2 shocks)
2. *Asparagus setaceus* (several)
3. *Davallia* or *Humata* hare's-foot fern
4. *Asplenium nidus* 'Curly'
5. *Cryptanthus fosterianus*
6. *Ficus benjamina* 'Too Little'
7. *Begonia* 'Dewdrop'

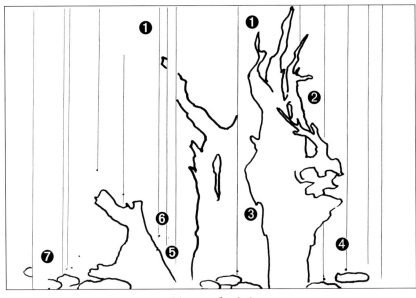

Diagram for 9-6

This piece could be altered to produce the effect of Magritte's Garden (page 131). Different pieces of wood would be needed—the pieces in Watchers are too compact and could not be sectioned in a way that suggests interrupted continuity. For this you need pieces with extended branches that spread horizontally. Such pieces are easy to find, and replicas are not hard to make. The pieces could then be sectioned and some of the sections discarded. The remaining sections would be positioned against the white boards. However, we think this piece already has a surreal quality. On the other hand, giving it a Magritte twist might heighten the effect significantly.

9-5 Watchers

9-6 Watchers (now in the company of more plants)

FLIGHT

These pieces (figures 9-7–9-10) were designed to fit a narrow, high space. We wanted the designs to be scale-independent and, just as our wall pieces suggest horizontal modularity (see figures 4-11 and 5-25), we wanted these to suggest vertical modularity, so that their height could be extended arbitrarily without an increase in their width. We could imagine such pieces reaching 20 ft (6 m) or more above the floor. On the other hand, strict modularity, in which the modules are identical, is a recipe for boredom. We were looking for designs that would allow variation from module to module.

The designs that we came up with use boards that stretch from floor to ceiling, regardless of the room's height. Not only do these boards create a strong vertical accent, but they also can be interpreted as trees in a forest. Painted white, they suggest a forest of aspen or birch. We affixed roots and branches to the boards at various heights, and it's these components that give the designs modularity with variation.

Staggering the floor placement of the boards and positioning the freeform elements so that some boards are behind them and some are in front of them creates an illusion of depth even within a few feet of space. Although they are photographed in landscape format, it is easy to imagine the designs extending to an arbitrary height.

As we set the pieces up, they seemed to accrue a certain elemental aspect, a primitive presence that surprised us. If we squinted and stepped back a little we could imagine that the suspended roots and branches were early creatures attempting flight.

Before There Were Birds

Before there were birds there were —what? Some people think there were bird-hipped dinosaurs, creatures with tiny pre-wing forelimbs that were too feeble for flight, too weak to grab, too frail to stand on. What could these creatures do

with these ridiculous appendages? Scratch their noses? Perhaps thumb them at Darwin? And where was the grand old granddad of evolution theory at this time? Out to lunch, apparently, while nature was selecting the unfittest of the unfit to soar above it all.

We do believe in evolution, but stories like this one—and there are quite a few of them—are a bit puzzling. The thought of clumsy bird-hipped dinosaurs hip-hopping through the forest, making a sorry attempt now and then to fly or at least glide, amuses us. And this is what was running through our minds as we developed this piece (figures 9-7 and 9-8).

Pieces of wood found on the floor of an old cottonwood grove played the role of our klutzy prebirds. We looked for pieces that were well weathered, well chewed by insects, and partly decomposed by mold—wood that was about to be digested by nature and used as sustenance for new trees. We carved these pieces up, stabilized them with

polyurethane resin, and hung them from the rafters or attached them to vertical panels. We tried our best to give them the appearance of flight. And they do seem to be wending their way through the board forest in fine fashion.

But, of course, the composition was our main concern—not a strange scientific exercise in the modeling of bird evolution. The two versions that we show here are quite similar, and we wonder if adding plants makes that much of a difference.

Plants in figure 9-8:
1. *Rhipsalis paradoxa* (3 shocks, top)
2. *Echeveria* hybrid (2)
3. *Euphorbia splendens* (3)
4. *Crassula perforata* (3 rear)
5. *Sempervivum* 'Alpine Rose' (several pots)
6. *Agave stricta*
7. *Aloe humilis*
8. *Haworthia xiphiophylla*
9. *Beaucarnea recurvata* (rear)

9-7 Before There Were Birds

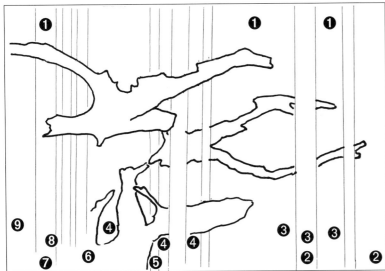

Diagram for 9-8

9-8 Before There Were Birds (with plants)

Taking Wing

This (figures 9-9 and 9-10) is yet another episode in our mock scientific saga on the evolution of birds. It is a gathering of prebirds trying to be birds. The wide body on the right with its arms raised is not going to fly, at least not yet. It may turn out to be a real turkey, or just a Spruce Goose (the giant wooden Hughes Aircraft airplane that never got off the ground). Probably it is nothing more than an evolutionary dead end. The creature to the left of it isn't faring much better. It's standing on one leg and has one arm raised, reaching for the sky but tragically never getting off the ground. True, it's leaner and maybe meaner than the others, but it, too, may be nothing more than another evolutionary dead end.

The remaining two show some promise. Peregrine falcons they're not, at least not yet. But one of them, though still not a sky walker, was nearly able to leave the frame of the picture. And its companion on the upper left is airborne. However, where it's going, it knows not—up and to our left, down and to our right, anything is possible.

We did this piece in two variations, the first (figure 9-9) without plants, the second (figure 9-10) with them. We leave it to the reader to choose which is more successful. Do the plants add interest to the scene by way of contrast in color, texture, and form? Or do they merely add confusion, a superfluous element that detracts from the clarity of the overall composition and diminishes its effect?

And what about the inane interpretations we laid on these two pieces? This type of free association when looking at an abstract design is usually nothing more than harmless fun. On the other hand, it is unlikely to lend insight, and it may get in the way of understanding what the piece is about or may offer. The more abstract the piece, the greater the possibility that an interpretation will be totally irrelevant, distracting, and misleading.

Plants in figure 9-10, clockwise from
    top right:
Davallia or *Humata*? (2)
Opuntia (3), wonderfully weird, but
    a magnet for mealybugs
Euphorbia tirucalli
Crassula argentea 'Golem' (2)
Euphorbia?, miniature, densely clus-
    tering
Asparagus setaceus asparagus fern

9-9 Taking Wing

9-10 Taking Wing (with plants)

TRIGGER WAITING FOR ROY ROGERS

A bit of whimsy in figures 9-11–9-13. Roy is off in the bushes somewhere doing who knows what. His trusty steed Trigger patiently awaits his return. Trigger is a slab of cottonwood bark that we found lying on the ground in a grove of weather-beaten patriarchs. Cottonwoods are short-lived trees of heroic proportions, and their bark is wonderfully textured with heavy corruga-

tions. Kept dry it seems to last forever, but a plastic coating would insure its longevity.

None of the plants used here would be at home on the range; they are from the wet tropics and would wither in anything approaching desert dryness, heat, or sun. However, most of them will be perfectly happy in indoor conditions.

We corralled three versions of

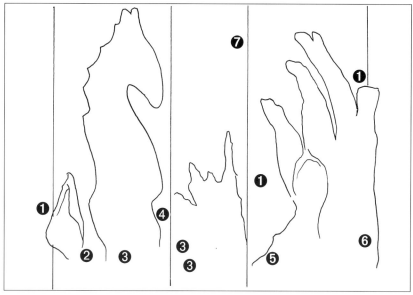

Diagram for 9-12

9-11 Trigger Waiting for Roy Rogers

this setup: one without plants (figure 9-11); one with a fairly full mix of plants (figure 9-12); and one with just a few rather modest plants (figure 9-13). Although the unplanted version certainly has some interest, we believe that the planted versions have much more. As to which of these we prefer, it's a toss-up—but the simpler treatment seems less canonical.

Plants in figure 9-12:
1. *Brassaia arboricola* 'Dwarf'
2. *Calathea makoyana*
3. *Cryptanthus fosterianus* (3)
4. *Billbergia* 'Fantasia'
5. *Begonia* 'Dewdrop'
6. *Aspidistra elatior* 'Milky Way'
7. *Platycerium elephantotis* (above, mounted on a slab of cork bark)

9-12 Trigger Waiting for Roy Rogers (with plants)

Plants in figure 9-13:
Tillandsia usneoides Spanish
   moss (several shocks on top)
Psilotum nudum (4)
Ficus pumila 'Quercifolia'

**9-13 Trigger Waiting for Roy
Rogers (variation)**

CAGED

The slab of wood we caged as the dominant feature of the composition in figures 9-14 and 9-15 was a lucky find. We came across it in a field about to be cleared for the construction of a shopping mall. A grove of giant trees once flourished there, and now their remains were scattered over an acre of land. We stumbled over our treasure half-buried in the soil, captured it, cleaned it, dried it, and did nothing else but live with it for a few months before deciding how to use it.

We stood the piece upright and leaned it against the wall. Using narrow slats of wood painted black, we pinned it in place, even passing some of the slats through openings in the piece. That seemed to confine the beast, but if it ever sends down roots into the floor, all bets are off.

The slats delineate the perimeters of the landscape and set it off from the surrounding space. The strict geometry of the cage is a strong counterpoint to the flowing, in some places writhing, lines of the beast. And this sets up just the kind of tension we love to express. The main compositional device of the arrangement is the juxtaposition of freeform elements with geometrically precise manufactured elements, and the effect does not depend on the specific nature of this piece of wood. All sorts of other shapes could be caged in this way to create an interesting setup. Still, we consider ourselves lucky to have captured this particular creature.

Figure 9-14 shows the creature alone in its bare cage—it's an unremittingly harsh effect. Placing plants around it, as in figure 9-15, moderates the harshness, but perhaps with some loss of power. Maybe for this arrangement, as in so many others, less is more.

Plants in figure 9-15:
1. *Rhipsalis paradoxa*
2. *Tillandsia seleriana*
3. *Nephrolepis exaltata* 'Dallas' dwarf cultivar of the Boston fern
4. *Rhipsalis capilliformis* old man's beard
5. *Brassaia arboricola* 'Dwarf'
6. *Asplenium nidus* 'Curly' (4)
7. *Brassaia arboricola* 'Variegated Dwarf'
8. *Aspidistra elatior* 'Milky Way'

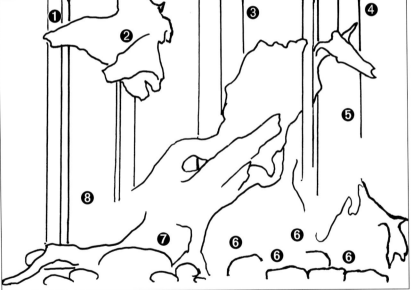

Diagram for 9-15

9-14 Caged

9-15 Caged (the presence of plants quiets the beast)

STEPPING OUT

The arrangement in figures 9-16 and 9-17 would be more cheerful if its main character weren't so macabre: A cloaked figure without a head steps menacingly through the columns, a dismounted, demented demon in search of Ichabod. The form certainly has presence, and not much is needed to present it forcefully: Give it center stage and let it assert itself. The addition of other strong elements to the design would only lessen the impact of the entire composition. However, the slats of wood play an important role. They define and isolate the space around the figure. Its dark color and free form stand in sharp contrast to the linearity of the black slats and stark whiteness of the background; the verticality of the slats emphasizes the height of the composition.

The field-wood figure is about 4 ft (1.2 m) tall and 4 ft (1.2 m) wide, and these dimensions determined the size of the entire piece. Were it three or four times larger, the piece would be that much more impressive. However, finding a natural wood figure of that size and the right character is not likely.

Of course, the general theme could be realized in any size by using a different form as the main feature. That form could be constructed from several pieces of wood or fabricated out of fiberglass, epoxy, or cement (see page 17). But we enjoy knowing that our fanciful figure is a natural object found lying in a field. It lends an additional level of interest to the design: the contrast of manmade forms and natural forms that we find so exciting.

The addition of plants to the piece (figure 9-17) dresses it up a bit, giving it a more completed look, but at the cost of reducing its monumentality. The wooden figure is still stepping out, but it appears wider, shorter, and less menacing.

Plants in figure 9-17, from left to right:
Brassaia arboricola 'Dwarf'
Zamia floridana
Calathea makoyana
Syngonium 'Dwarf'
Zamia furfuracea
Geranium hybrid, succulent geranium
Rhipsalis paradoxa (above right)

9-16 Stepping Out

9-17 Stepping Out: Into the forest

BACKSTAGE WITH THE FAMED CALLIGRAPHIC ACROBATS OF CHINA

Leaning against the pillars backstage are the famed calligraphic acrobats of China (figures 9-18 and 9-19). They're resting, but they're wired. The taut, lean, zigzag bodies can barely contain their dynamism. Come curtain call, they'll tumble, jump, and fly, releasing all that pent-up energy.

These are the same wooden figures shown in figures 6-1 and 6-2. But there they are elevated and in contact with one another—the composition is more active and movement is implied. These versions poise the figures in a none-too-stable equilibrium, but nevertheless they are standing still.

The plants also play a role. In the earlier piece, the larger plants with their gently curved branches soften the arrangement and suggest mo-

tion. In this piece, the plants have a more emphatic and individualistic role, their contrast with the other elements is more striking, and they add to the static quality of the piece.

Why did we place that piece there and this piece here? The more dominant role of the plants and the use of lattice in the first piece argued for its interpretation as a garden. The boards of indeterminate height in this piece need a ceiling to define their length, and a ceiling does not suggest a garden. So we put it here.

Both designs can be extended vertically or horizontally into wall

pieces. Of course, adding wood figures higher up on the boards of the piece shown here would destroy some of its static character, but it is quite likely to work on its own terms. The spirit of the first piece would not change at all. Many variations on this theme are possible, and the acrobats can be counted on to give each new performance a special twist.

Plants in figure 9-19, clockwise
    from upper left:
Aeranges hybrid
Codonanthe crassifolia
Alocasia 'Black Velvet'
Cryptanthus hybrid
Paphiopedilum Maudiae 'Magnificum'
Alocasia Amazonica (2)
Cryptanthus hybrid
Cryptanthus fosterianus

9-18 Backstage with the Famed Calligraphic Acrobats of China

9-19 The calligraphic acrobats surrounded backstage by the leafy tributes of their devoted fans

RED BANNER

9-20 Red Banner

This piece is about design. We wanted to introduce a strong note of color and explore sharp contrasts in texture, form, and rhythm, as well as between natural and manufactured elements. We had no preconceived theme, no intended allusions, and no story to tell. The piece is not supposed to be representational in any way.

Nothing that moves us strongly is easily ignored or forgotten, and we are strongly moved by the art of the Orient, particularly by the garden arts of China and Japan: ikebana and bonsai. Some of these influences show through in this piece.

The background, looking like pale marble, is an array of acoustic ceiling panels. Such panels are available in many textures and colors and can be purchased from construction-supply outlets. The lattice was purchased at a local nursery, and we painted it black. The red banner is a strip of cloth.

Plants in figure 9-20, clockwise from upper left:
Geranium hybrid (3), the succulent leaves of these cut
    stems will last for months in a container of water
    under these conditions
Tillandsia usneoides Spanish moss
Codonanthe crassifolia
Chlorophytum comosum '
    Mandaianum'
Aglaomorpha or *Drynaria*? (2)
Cryptanthus fosterianus

CANYON SUITE

Until they drop off steeply into the Pacific, ridge after ridge of land separates the successive canyons of the Na Pali Cliffs on the northwest coast of the Hawaiian island of Kauai. Most of these giant, narrow flanges are fully carpeted in brilliant green jungle. But other sections, where the cliffs fall off into the sea even more sharply, have surfaces more freshly eroded down to the naked dirt and stone. These cliffs are red, black, or gray in color.

Ridges even more precipitous rise from the desert floor along Devil's Garden Trail in Arches National Park, Utah. Hundreds of feet tall, arranged in staggered rows and columns, and all in the same orientation, they are called the Fins; but to us, the formation looks much more like a regatta of yachts in full sail. The entire landscape of sand and rock is a vibrant red-brown—surreal against a deep blue sky.

The same effect can be seen in buff and gray at Grand Wash in Utah's Capitol Reef National Park. Here the canyon walls are so precipitous and so winding that a sudden downpour puts hikers at risk of being swept away by a flash flood. And the deeper you enter the canyon, the steeper and closer the sides become, until you can touch both simultaneously and the threat becomes palpable.

But no such threat is felt on the east rim of the Glacier Creek Canyon on the approach to Mills Lake in Rocky Mountain National Park, Colorado (figure 9-21). This is one of our favorite hikes in this glorious park. Looking across the river to the opposite wall, we see what seems to be a succession of ridges, appearing as flat panels of gray stone, compressed one upon the other into a two-dimensional frieze. Here and there you do see some greenery and an occasional snag rising from the narrow banks in front of the cliff. Perhaps it is this scene more than any other that we had in mind when we designed the piece in figures 9-22–9-24.

The canyon walls in the set are the panels that make up our Maligne Canyon background. Gray- and black-painted wood panels complete the setting. Small rectangles of black-painted wood placed on the floor of the piece and black-painted stones on the ground suggest a riverbed.

The first view of the piece (figure 9-22) shows only the infrastructure. Perhaps it's strong enough to stand on its own, but we think it needs the presence of plants to complete it.

For the second version (figure 9-23), we used various tropical plants to furnish the infrastructure. All are easy to grow, and all are easy to find except for the spotted cast-iron plant, *Aspidistra elatior* 'Milky Way,' seen near the center of the arrangement. Finding this plant requires a bit of a search, but one of the specialty firms listed in the source index should carry it. Of course, there are many suitable substitutions for this plant as well as for the others.

Plants in figure 9-23, clockwise from upper left:
Rhipsalis paradoxa
Codonanthe crassifolia
Nephrolepis exaltata 'Dallas,' dwarf cultivar of the Boston fern

Adiantum raddianum 'Sea Foam' (another to the left of center)
Aspidistra elatior 'Milky Way'
Ficus pumila 'Variegata' (3)
Selaginella?

The third version (figure 9-24) is a compromise between the first two. To our eyes, it has a spare quality that imparts a bit of mystery to the scene, but it does not have the unfinished look of the first version. It's our favorite. We can picture this piece as the entrance to a hallway or a courtyard. Maybe the panels are placed far enough apart from each other so that the space between them could be used as corridors leading off to the sides. Alternatively, the piece could be seen as part of a wall or extended in a modular fashion to make an entire wall.

Plants in figure 9-24:
Codonanthe crassifolia (top)
Microsorum punctatum 'Cristatum Dwarf'
Ficus pumila 'Variegata'

9-21 A succession of stone slabs on the approach to Mills Lake,
Rocky Mountain National Park, Colorado

9-22 Canyon Suite

9-23 Canyon Suite (with plants)

9-24 Canyon Suite (variation)

PART THREE

Drawings

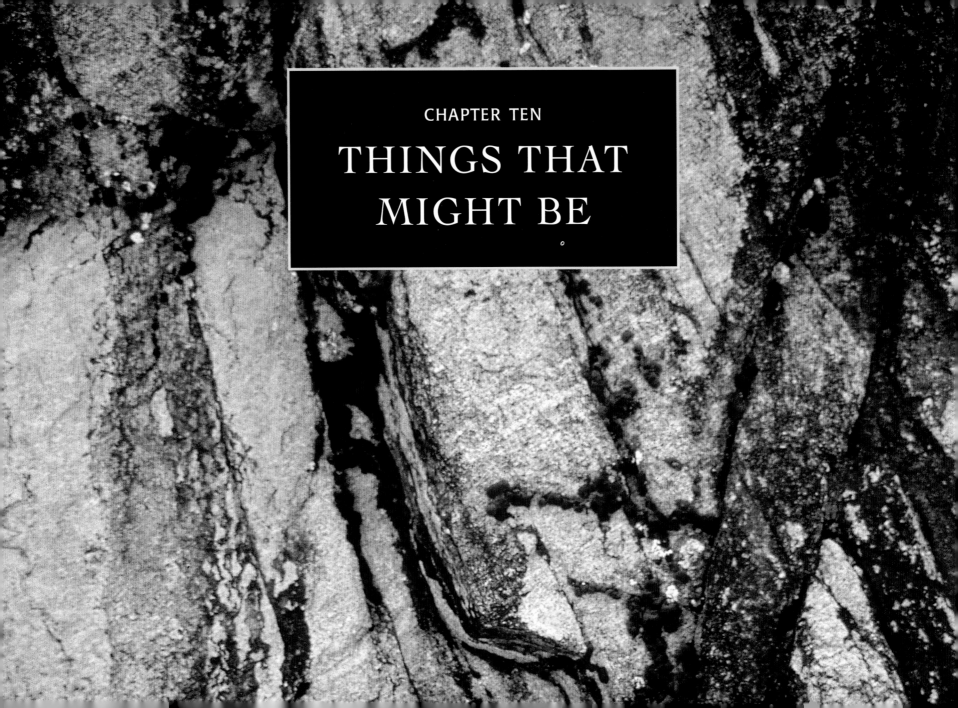

CHAPTER TEN

THINGS THAT
MIGHT BE

All sorts of things can inspire a landscape design, and different designers are inspired by different things. Even when two designers tap into the same source, they might differ in what they get from it. But certain things are more likely to spur the imagination than others. Painting, sculpture, and architecture offer all sorts of ideas for interior landscapes—not only overall composition and formal devices, but also expressive content. Outdoor gardens have a lot to offer, and even miniature landscapes and arrangements as seen in bonsai and ikebana can provide ideas. Manufactured items also contribute to our visual language, introducing forms and textures associated with industry and technology. Incorporating such items into an otherwise naturalistic design often adds surprise and excitement to the piece.

The landscapes of nature may be the richest source of ideas for interior landscapes. In nature one finds an endless variety of forms, colors, and compositions. Maybe it is our response to nature's designs that heightens our awareness of the potential for expressive power of landscapes designed by people.

Even when a likely source of inspiration turns out to be a dud, it may aid the designer in sharpening his or her own aesthetic. One could argue that many of the major innovations in art have come as reactions against the norms of the time.

With this wonderful abundance of sources, the problem becomes one of recording them. How do you capture such sources for future access? Photography may be the most convenient tool to capture an image for further reference. But for modifying images, for combining them in complicated ways, and for rendering images seen only in the imagination, nothing takes the place of drawing.

The drawings in this chapter are a collection of some of the many in our files. These drawings are always casual—*sketches* is a better term for them—and are not meant to stand on their own. Rather, their interest lies in the effectiveness of the landscape they suggest. They are hand-drawn with simple materials on whatever scrap of paper happens to be on hand when the urge to draw strikes.

Most of the sketches are summarily relegated to the trashcan. A few are given a temporary stay of sentence and then upon later review are chucked. But a few remain in our files for a long time. Some of these designs are eminently realizable; some are ambitious; some are just plain silly but nevertheless hold a shred of a worthwhile idea. All the designs could be realized in a variety of ways, with various materials.

Water Features

Water—it brings a landscape to life. Its sparkle, music, and kaleidoscopic fragmentation of colors all contribute to the effect. But you don't need to recreate an actual stream to get the effect of water. Instead, water can simply be suggested (see figures 4-1, 8-6, and 8-12). In the pieces shown in Part II, we intentionally decided to take on the challenge of capturing some of the effects of water without actually using it in the design. This is not a new idea. For centuries, Chinese and Japanese masters of landscape design have been creating landscapes that give the impression of being rich in water features but have no water in them whatsoever (see figure 2-1). In some of these works you are led to imagine a stream meandering through a mountain meadow, in others you see a waterfall or cascade where there is only patterned rock carefully arranged to create the effect. There are even examples where an ocean scene is suggested, complete with mountains emerging from the depths and waves washing on the shore. A dry landscape that conjures up images of water is perfectly magical.

Nevertheless, we are itching to start a series of setups featuring real water, and we have made many drawings (figures 10-1–10-4) that use moving water as a dominant component. But we also like still water, water in clear reflecting ponds, and black water in ponds that looks like polished onyx. We even like water when it's suspended as a mist above which plants, rocks,

10-1

the first three examples. Artificial stone should be given preference over real stone because of the difference in weight and the potential to customize forms. Cast aluminum or bronze would be perfect for the piece in figure 10-4, although fiberglass or ceramic might also work. The more massive slabs indicated in figure 10-3 would be best realized in cast stone. Even if the slabs of the last two pieces are very thin, epi-phytic orchids, ferns, cacti, and philodendrons could be attached to the surface over a pad of long-fibered sphagnum moss. Crevices for planting could be molded into the thicker slabs.

There is no shortage of plants that love water and would be apt additions to these pieces. Some of these plants like having only their feet wet, others want a cool mist to surround them, and there are even

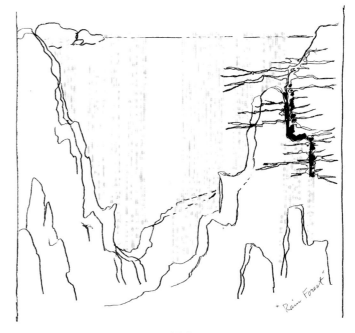

10-2

and branches seem to float. This effect is easily obtained with commercial miniature foggers that create a mist by atomizing water with ultrasonic vibrations and operate for pennies a day. Many other effects of moving water, such as streams, cascades, and waterfalls, are also easily created by using small water pumps.

All of these designs occupy very little space from front to back, although their vertical and horizontal dimensions can be quite large. This makes them appropriate wall pieces, although those in figures 10-3 and 10-4 might work best as free-standing pieces with the water cascading into a shallow basin.

Stone is the main component of

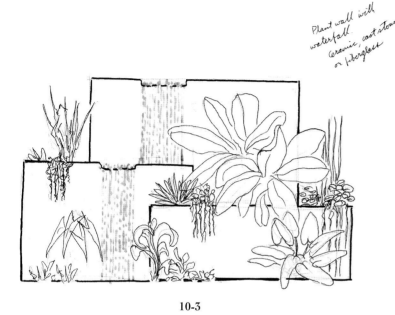

Plant wall with waterfall. Ceramic, cast stone, or fiberglass

10-3

offer a fragmented view of the other side. This allows objects and movements behind the panels to contribute to the overall effect.

Figures 10-8 and 10-9 need some explanation—there are a couple of ways to interpret them. In both interpretations the shaded areas are to be seen as cutout regions. Bands of varying widths border these regions. In one interpretation, these are ridges that protrude from the flat surface toward the viewer. In the other interpretation, they are the beveled edges of the cutouts.

All of the panel designs incorporate treelike forms. Placing several side by side gives the effect of an abstract forest fragment. Some of the cutouts are fairly naturalistic representations of tree shadows (figures 10-5 and 10-7); others abstract the rhythms of tree forms (figures 10-6, 10-8, and 10-9). When not

those that want to be entirely submerged. Always check a plant's culture requirements before using it in a setup.

Screens and Partitions

Sometimes you might want to screen off part of a room for privacy or to create a space for some special task. The space might have to be reconfigured every so often, or maybe the division of the space is to be permanent but erecting a wall to enclose it would be impractical or destroy the room's spaciousness. Or maybe you want to divide the floor plan to redirect traffic or simply to add more interest to the space.

In such situations a set of panels might provide the best means of dividing the room. Figures 10-5–10-9 suggest such sets of panels. The panels are flat and are designed to be seen from both sides. The designs are open, with each panel having large cutout sections that

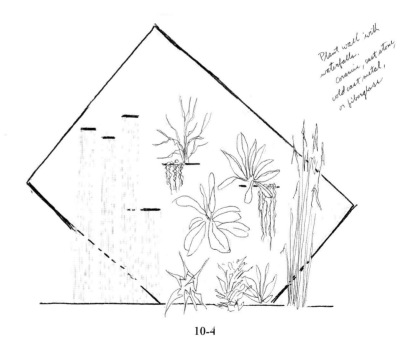

Plant wall with waterfalls. Ceramic, cast stone, cold cast metal, or fiberglass

10-4

208

needed, the panels can be stored in a very small space. Alternatively, they can be regrouped in a less rigid arrangement to give a more three-dimensional representation of a forest.

In figure 10-5, tree forms flow from panel to panel, with the flow paradoxically interrupted by empty space. Perhaps it brings to mind Magritte's painting *Carte blanche*, described in chapter 6. The tree forms in the panel can be painted black or modified a bit and rendered as perforations. A three-dimensional Magritte effect can be obtained in other ways using living plant material and panels as described on page 130.

The panels can be made out of a variety of materials: wood, plastic (opaque or transparent), ceramic fiberglass, or aluminum. The panels in figures 10-8 and 10-9 might be best in aluminum or brushed stainless steel.

Backgrounds and Walls

The pieces in figures 10-10–10-12 are essentially bas-reliefs and have been designed to be seen from one side only, positioned against a wall or actually forming a wall. However, the piece in figure 10-12 can also be seen as a freestanding panel that can be viewed from both sides. The perforations are large enough to glimpse activity on the other side but not large enough to offer a clear view—a ploy to add a bit of life and mystery to the piece.

The rock walls shown in figures 10-10 and 10-11 can be fashioned out of ceramic, concrete, fiberglass, or real rock. There is nothing new about making walls in this way. In fact, rock-textured panels are widely available in 4-by-8-ft (1.2-by-2.5-m) sheets. The patterns of these panels are intentionally modular, so panels can be joined to create a long wall. Some of these panels are so realistic that you have to examine them quite closely to avoid being fooled. However, the patterns of the commercial sheets are homogenous enough to be really boring. So we tried to bring some rhythm to the arrangement, to give the design some sweep, to indicate the potential motion found so frequently in nature. We wanted to suggest a rock-

10-5

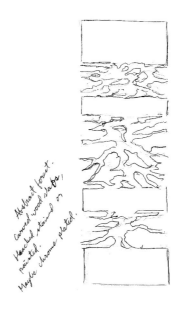 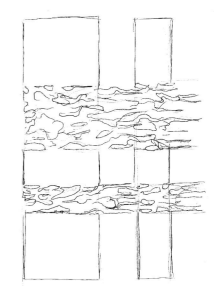

10-6

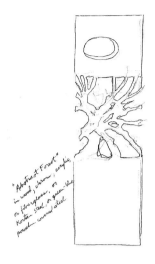
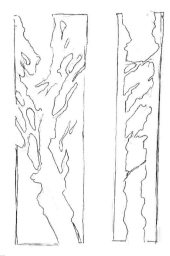

"Abstract Forest" in wood, chrome, acrylic or fiberglass, or Korten steel, or green-like powder-coated steel

10-7

slide in the making, a formation full of potential energy.

All of these walls can be left bare or furnished with plants by tucking their roots into the interstices between the rocks. All sorts of plants will work—ferns, gesneriads, and epiphytic cacti would be among our first choices. The walls also can be used as backdrops for groups of plants. The plants can be placed in pots or stone troughs to suggest an extension of the rockfall onto a boulder field. Alternatively, the containers can be chosen to be as small as possible, and then hidden by rocks and pebbles.

Nature provides an endless variety of models to inspire a wall (see figures 10-13–10-15). Some more examples can be seen in figures 2-2–2-4. These drawings show just a few of the possible interpretations.

Canyons, Passes, and Foothills Wall Pieces

The designs in figures 10-16–10-20 are meant to be placed against

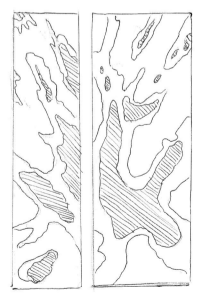

10-8

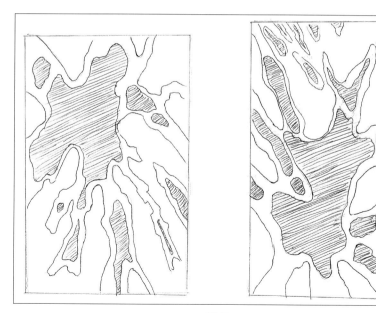

10-9

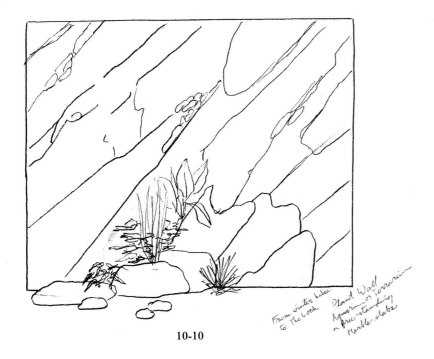

From winter hike to the Loch

Plant Wall for Aquarium or terrarium or free-standing on Marble slabs

10-10

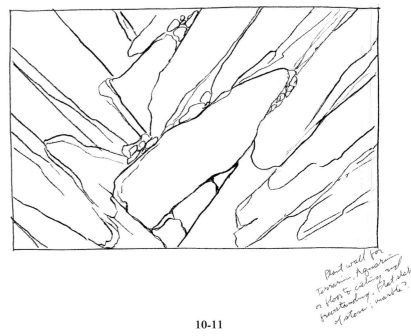

Plant wall for Terrarium, Aquarium or floor to ceiling and freestanding. Flat slabs of stone, marble?

10-11

walls. Each uses a succession of panels to create the illusion of depth, but the pieces occupy very little floor space from front to back. However, the designs in figures 10-19 and 10-20 suggest shorter and more sprawling pieces that could also be set up as freestanding sculptures viewed from all sides.

The pieces in figures 10-16–10-18 can be seen as canyon walls or passes through the foothills. The arrangement of planes and boulders seem to indicate a path upward along switchbacks leading to the higher ridges. The contrast between the dark boulders and light panels, and between naturalistic elements and manufactured elements, creates an exciting visual tension. Several of our setups explore this theme (see figures 7-4, 7-6, 7-10, and 9-22). In fact, some of the landscapes in chapter 7 are similar to the sketches shown here (compare figure 10-16 with figure 7-4, for example).

Plants can be incorporated into these designs. In the setup pictured in figure 7-4, we used painted branches, which would be ideal in the pieces suggested by these sketches. But living plants could also be used. In particular, groves of small fig trees would work quite well. However, this may be one of those cases where less is more, and the bare bones version has the greatest impact.

Each of the pieces sketched here can be realized in a variety of different materials. Rocks can be natural or artificial (see page 18) and painted if need be. The panels in figures 10-16 and 10-17 can be cut out of

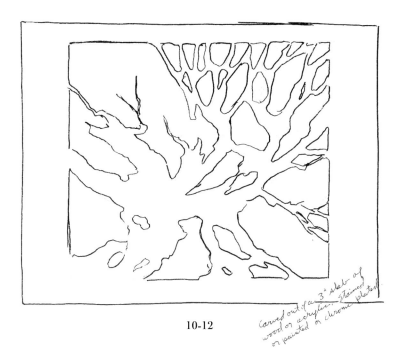

10-12

Carved out of a 3" slab of wood or acrylic. Stained or painted or chrome plated.

10-13 Canyon wall on Glacier Gorge; Rocky Mountain National Park, Colorado

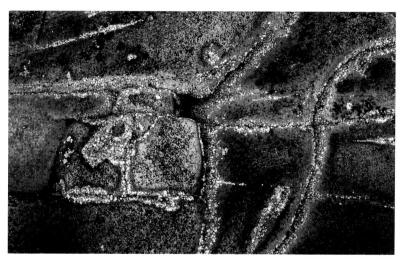

10-14 Bottom of a tide pool, Acadia National Park, Maine

Masonite, Sheetrock, plywood, or various other materials—then textured if desired and painted. They might be tiled or made out of ceramic. They could be planked as was done in several of the landscapes in chapter 7 (see figures 7-4 and 7-6).

The same approach could be used to realize the designs of figures 10-19 and 10-20. However, here our first choice would be slate or black marble for the dark panels and brushed aluminum or stainless steel for the light panels. In figure 10-18, we think of the wall as being made out of sheets of stainless steel or aluminum, polished in this case, and either flat or curved.

We had no particular scale in mind for these pieces, but we think that a large realization—say, one to two stories tall—of the designs in figures 10-16–10-18 would be more effective than a small one. Those in

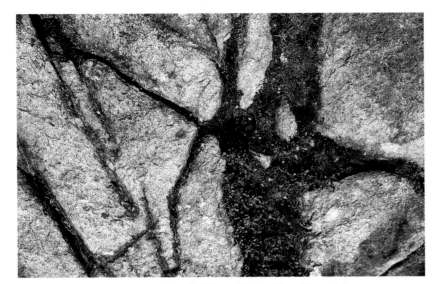

10-15 Fractured wall, Mount Major, New Hampshire

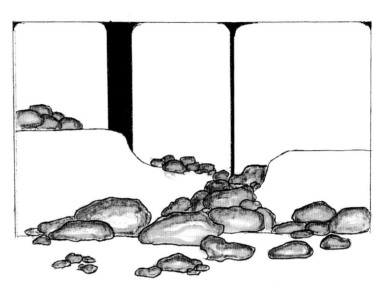

10-16

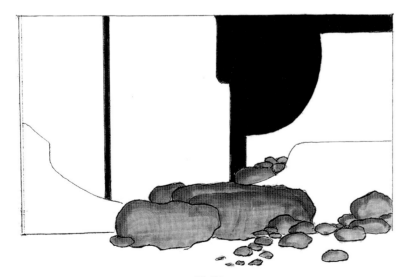

10-17

10-18

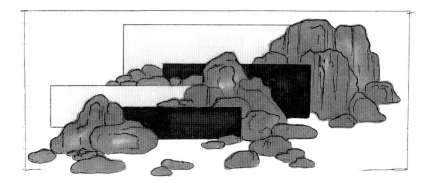

10-19

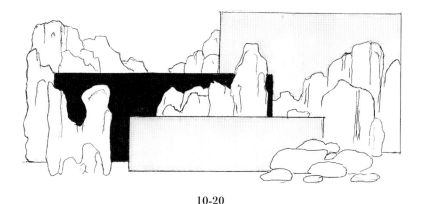

10-20

figures 10-19 and 10-20 could be realized effectively at a height between 4 ft (1.2 m) and 6 ft (1.8 m). In a larger size, they might appear clumsy.

Plant Frames and Hanging Gardens

A plant frame (figures 10-21–10-29) is a flat structure of rather open design that is freestanding or suspended on a wall or against a window. Plants are then attached to it, making a sort of two-dimensional living tapestry, a hanging garden. Seeing it as a canyon wall festooned with plants justifies calling it a landscape.

Furnishing a plant frame is easy. After all, life high in the trees is the lifestyle of choice for many plants in the jungles of the tropics. You can choose from epiphytic bromeliads, cacti, ferns, gesneriads, and orchids. There are even tree-dwelling rhododendrons and several kinds of carnivorous plants that will serve the purpose. Just among the bromeliads and orchids alone are thousands of candidates, and among them are some of the most magnificent plants on the planet.

But if limiting your choice to the true epiphytes is too constraining, all sorts of terrestrials can be persuaded to try life on a plant frame. An inconspicuous pot filled with a water-retentive mix is often all that is needed, and even this can be neatly concealed with a bit of Spanish moss.

Maintenance can be as challenging or as simple as you wish—it all depends on the site and the choice of plants. Misting once a week with a very diluted fertilizer will be enough care for most epiphytic cacti, many epiphytic ferns and bromeliads, and even some orchids. Other plants, especially when placed in a room with humidity below 40%, will require daily misting.

Choosing plants with moderate light requirements will avert many problems, and supplemental lighting from ceiling fixtures can be arranged to cover shortfalls. Phototropism can be a problem with some plants when they are grown next to a window: The plant will grow toward the window, leaning away from the viewer, which is not what you want. However, if the plant is mounted properly to the frame you will be able to periodically remove it from the frame, rotate it, and remount it with little effort. An even more expedient way to counter phototropism is to rotate the entire frame 180 degrees (although this may be difficult with very large-scale frames). Many of the epiphytes are slow-growing and

10-21

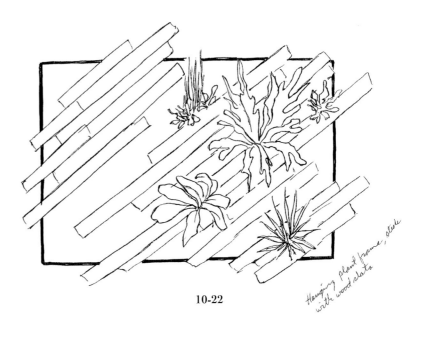

10-22

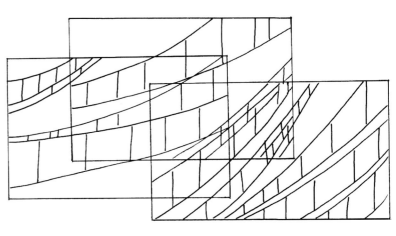

10-23

need rotation only once every six months or so.

Several kinds of plant frames are pictured here: slatted frames, wire frames, and frames made out of branches. All are easy to construct, and all use materials that are inexpensive and easy to find.

The slatted frames (figures 10-21 and 10-22) are just that—wooden slats affixed to a circular or rectangular frame of metal. Wood could also be used for the frames. We see the frames as painted black and the wood as being painted, stained, or bleached to whatever color is needed. Of course, the color needed has to complement the color of the sur-

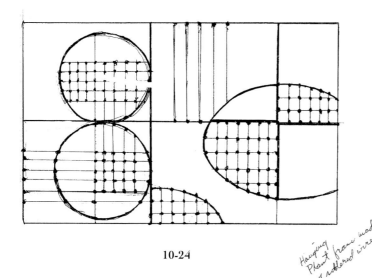

10-24

*Hanging
Plant frame made
of soldered wire.*

roundings and the plants that will be attached to the frames. Without plants, these pieces are a bit too spare to be considered complete.

The wire frames are soldered or welded constructions using wire or metal rods. The piece shown in figure 10-23 consists of three rectangular frames, each of which could be displayed alone. However, grouping them adds complexity and makes for a more interesting piece.

The design shown in figure 10-24 was taken from a photograph of a microscope slide stage, a device that facilitates counting cells and organisms on a slide.

Figures 10-25–10-27 are designs for freestanding frames. Note that figure 10-27 is more or less the frame in figure 10-25 superimposed on that in figure 10-26. Again, the individual frames work on their own, but nesting the two makes a richer composition. When we designed these pieces, we were thinking of the cloudbursts we experienced in Caracas, Venezuela, where the raindrops are so

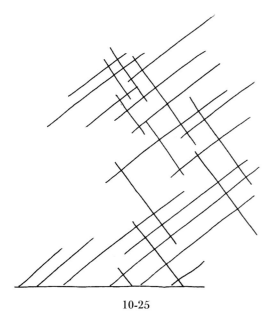

10-25

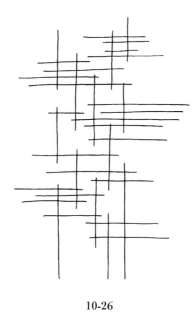

10-26

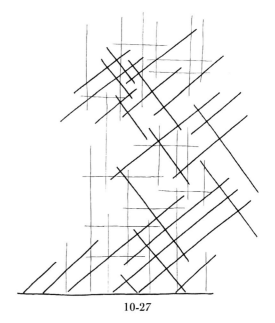

10-27

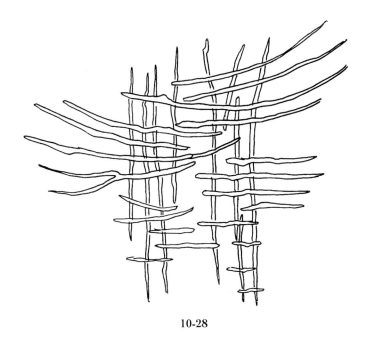

10-28

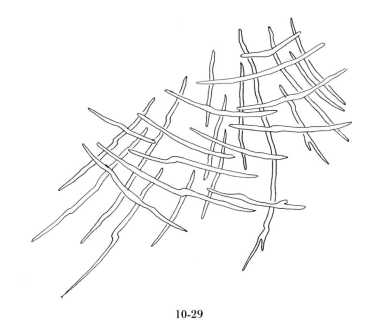

10-29

thick and travel so fast that they appear to be glass rods—"sticks of rain" our hosts called them. Every afternoon without fail the land was pelted with these "sticks of rain." Often the cloudburst was accompanied by wind, sometimes gentle enough to be called a breeze, but other times near hurricane force. Directed by the wind, the rain sometimes fell vertically but other times fell at such an angle as to appear horizontal. It was this effect that we had in mind when we designed these pieces. We tried to capture the random, ethereal aspect of the rain by a seemingly random (although parallel) distribution of the rods, leaving relatively few to establish connections and make the piece rigid.

The frames made out of branches (figures 10-28 and 10-29) can be assembled in several different ways. Fine wire (stainless steel is best) can fasten the branches together quickly and easily. Nylon fishing line can be used to tie the branches together and makes a strong but nearly invisible joint. Of course, the branches can be glued together. But our favorite method is to tie them together with polyethylene cord. The cord looks like hemp, but it lasts forever. We do nothing to conceal the ties—they add interest to the piece.

Ladders and Caged Branches

The pieces in figures 10-30–10-32 are from a series closely related to our plant frames and hanging gardens, in particular to the frames made out of branches. But here, the branches are much more substantial and have more character as individual components, particularly those in the caged branches series (figures 10-31 and 10-32). Finding branches interesting enough to be caged is

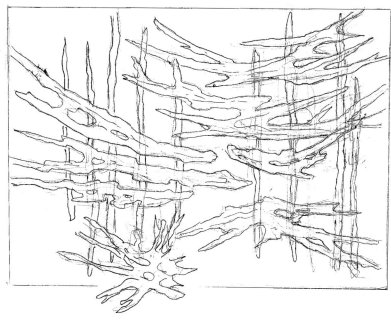

10-30

much more difficult than finding branches for the plant frames. But if they can't be found, they can always be pieced together from smaller branches.

Of course, both the ladder and the caged branches can be thought of as plant frames and furnished with plants. Groups of plants in containers, placed off center, would complement these pieces very well.

And a big, bold staghorn fern (*Platycerium*) or two, maybe along with shanks of chain-link cacti (*Rhipsalis paradoxa*), mounted to the ladder piece would be a nice addition. This would give the piece a stronger allusion to a landscape, or perhaps a vignette of landscape—say, a view into the forest canopy. But these pieces are more sculptural than the simple frames and can

stand on their own without plants more easily.

The ladder piece is meant to be suspended against a wall; the caged branches are intended to be free-standing and several of them can be grouped together. The wood can be bleached, stained, or painted. The size of these pieces is arbitrary, but we think of the cages as being 6 to 9 ft (1.8 to 2.7 m) tall, and the ladder at least that large.

Driftwood

Driftwood that has been snatched up by the sea, flayed free of its bark by the sand and waves, bleached bone white by the sun, and then tossed on the beach by the tide can hold its own as sculpture with ease (figure 10-33). Often the form that results is alive with jagged energy and seems to have more of the spirit of a wild animal than of a tree.

Usually these tree sculptures are thrown onto the shore in a pile like so much flotsam and jetsam. But sometimes a piece is deposited on rocks and lodges there where the sea cannot retrieve it. We have seen

driftwood wedged between massive blocks of black granite in a striking contrast of color, texture, and form. The wood seems to writhe against the stone in an attempt to break free. But nothing will move it for a long, long time. It's a stable landscape, yet one charged with energy. These are the landscapes we had in mind when we made the series of sketches from which figures 10-34–10-37 are taken.

The first two were designed to make the most out of contrasts—contrasts in black and white, and in aggressive, free form against static, geometric form. Tree forms like these are easy to find. We have dug them up in our own garden, we have found them in fields and construction sites, and they usually can be purchased where landscape materials are found. Of course, if nature can't provide you with the exact shape you want, a piece can be carved, several pieces can be joined together, or the entire form can be sculpted in a variety of materials (see page 17). Painted wood would suffice for the rectilinear elements of the design, but they could

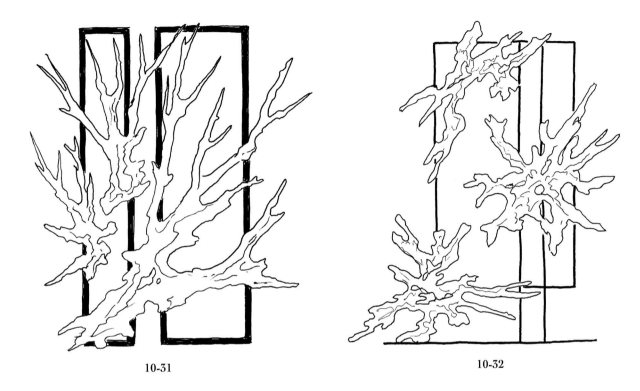

10-31

10-32

also be fashioned out of sheets of stone, ceramic, or metal.

The sketch shown in figure 10-37 has a somewhat different character, perhaps more closely related to our caged pieces in figures 10-31 and 10-32. Here, a root form is tied to bamboo poles and suspended well above the floor. The potential energy of the massive form compared to

the seemingly insubstantial poles gives the piece its visual tension. But bamboo poles are famously strong, and a piece like that in the sketch, if securely tied to the poles, would be there to stay.

Sun Stones, Moon Stones

In the wild one can find river boulders rolled and abraded into

almost-perfect spheres, granite cleaved into rectangular blocks, and sandstone shaped into freestanding forms that seem anything but the result of natural forces.

Ancient cultures around the world were intrigued by such expressions of nature, and they collected examples that impressed them the most. Often they trans-

ported these finds great distances and placed them so as to magnify their visual impact as much as possible. Sometimes they carved them to accentuate their form or to decorate them, and sometimes they placed them in groups or against architecture, creating arrangements still more powerful than the individual pieces.

The most elemental forms—spheres, discs, and rectangular blocks—are seen most often. Perhaps the first two derive their power from associations with the sun or moon, but how does one explain the blocks? Maybe they just satisfy the eye and mind or calm the spirit with their symmetry and predictability. These forms work on us in this way, and we return to them again and again. But to bring some variety into the composition, we scar, fracture, and partition the pieces before organizing the sections and fragments into a landscape.

The piece in figure 10-38 is such a design—an interior landscape 8 or 10 ft (2.5 or 3 m) tall placed between two walls at the end of a

10-33 A huge root washed up on the West Coast of South Island, New Zealand

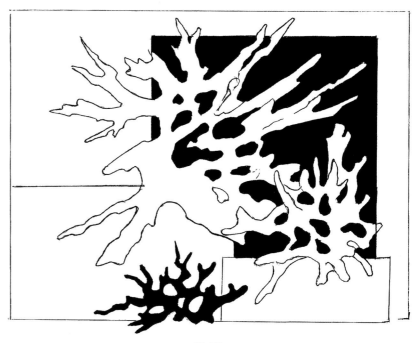

10-35

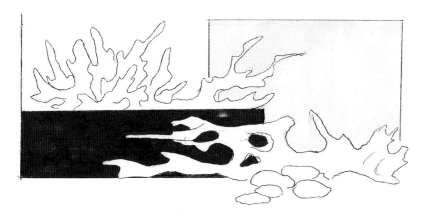

10-34

corridor. The side walls are needed to delineate the horizontal extent of the piece and make sense out of the quarter disc at the lower right. The forms are too massive to be carved out of rock or cast in solid concrete. However, light, sturdy, artificial rock can be made (see page 18). Plants are not necessary, but some could be displayed in pots posi-tioned on the floor. The piece would set them off to good effect, and their form and color would complement the rock.

This piece confuses the distinc-tion between landscape design, sculpture, and architecture, but that is part of its point—to reveal the distinction as arbitrary and per-haps unnecessary.

10-36 Bamboo on the Waimoku Falls Trail, Maui, Hawaii

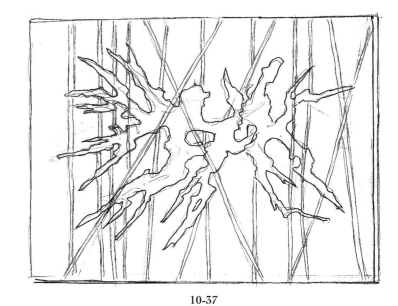

10-37

10-38

SOURCES FOR TROPICAL PLANTS AND HORTICULTURAL SUPPLIES

The World Wide Web has made finding whatever plants and horticulture supplies you need or desire vastly easier—you always can find a nursery-dot-com to serve you. These enterprises come and go, and presently there are far too many to list here. However, without making any endorsements or criticisms, here are some sources we have used.

Bloomfield Orchids
251 W. Bloomfield Road
Pittsford, NY 14534
•Slipper orchids

Brussel's Bonsai Nursery, Inc.
8365 Center Hill Road
Olive Branch, MS 38654
•Bonsai plants and materials, including pots and trays

California Carnivores
7020 Trenton-Healdsburg Road
Forestville, CA 95436
•Carnivorous plants

Carter and Holmes Orchids
629 Mendenhall Road, P.O. Box 668
Newberry, SC 09108
•Orchids and some other tropical plants

Charley's
17979 State Route 536
Mount Vernon, WA 98273
www.charleysgreenhouse.com
•Greenhouse and garden supplies

Fantasy Orchids, Inc.
830 W. Cherry Street
Louisville, CO 80027
www.fantasyorchids.com
•Orchids

Glasshouse Works
Church Street, P.O. Box 97
Stewart, OH 45778
www.glasshouseworks.com
•Tropical plants and succulents

Holladay Jungle
P.O. Box 5727 E.
Fresno, CA 93755
•Tillandsias

Hoosier Orchid Company
8440 West 82 Street
Indianapolis, IN 46278
•Orchids

H&R Nurseries, Inc.
41-240 Hihimanu Street
Waimanalo, HI 96795
•Orchids

J&L Orchids
20 Sherwood Road
Easton, CT 06612
•Miniature orchids

Kartuz Greenhouses
1408 Sunset Drive, P.O. Box 790
Vista, CA 92085
•Gesneriads, begonias, and other exotics

Logee's Greenhouses
141 North Street
Danielson, CT 06239
www.logees.com
•Tropical and subtropical plants

Michael's Bromeliads
1365 Canterbury Road N.
St. Petersburg, FL 33710
•Bromeliads

Northridge Gardens
9821 White Oak Avenue
Northridge, CA 91325
•Succulents

Oak Hill Gardens, Inc.
37 W. 550 Binnie Road
Dundee, IL 60118
•Orchids

OFE International
P.O. Box 161302
Miami, FL 33116
•Supplies for horticulture

Orchids by Hausermann
2 N. 134 Addison Road
Villa Park, IL 60181
www.orchidsbyhausermann.com
•Orchids

Orchids Limited
4630 N. Fernbrook Lane
Plymouth, MN 55446
•Orchids

Rod McLellan Company
914 S. Claremont Street
San Mateo, CA 94402
www.rodmclellan.com
•Orchids

Tropiflora
3530 Tallevast Road
Sarasota, FL 34243
www.tropiflora.com
•Bromeliads, orchids, succulents, exotics

Timber Press
133 S. W. Second Avenue, Suite 450
Portland, OR 97204
•Books on plants and horticulture

Also on the Web with links to suppliers of plants and growing materials are the following:

American Fern Society, www.amerfernsoc.org
American Orchid Society, www.orchidweb.org
Bromeliad Society International, www.bsi.org
Cactus and Succulent Plant Mall, www.cactus-mall.com
Cactus and Succulent Society of America, www.cssainc.org

BIBLIOGRAPHY

This is a brief list of books about indoor plants and their care. These books cover most of the plants that we have used as well as many others that are of potential value to the designer of interior landscapes.

Clarke, Charles. *Nepenthes of Borneo*. Sabah, Malaysia: Natural History Publications, 1997.

D'Amato, Peter. *The Savage Garden*. Berkeley: Ten Speed Press, 1998.

Elbert, Virginie F., and George A. Elbert. *Foliage Plants for Decorating Indoors*. Portland, OR: Timber Press, 1989.

Graf, Alfred B. *Exotica 5*. East Rutherford, NJ: Rohrs Co., 1976.

Hewitt, Terry. *Cacti and Succulents*. New York: DK Publishing, 1993.

Isley, Paul T. *Tillandsia*. Gardena, CA: Botanical Press, 1987.

Jones, David L. *Encyclopedia of Ferns*. Portland, OR: Timber Press, 1987.

Mabberley, D. J. *The Plant Book*. New York: Cambridge University Press, 1990.

McQueen, Jim, and Barbara McQueen. *Miniature Orchids*. Melbourne, Australia: The Text Publishing Company, 1992.

Pizzetti, Mariella. *Cacti and Succulents*. New York: Simon and Schuster, 1986.

Pridgeon, Alec. *The Illustrated Encyclopedia of Orchids*. Portland, OR: Timber Press, 1992.

Rowley, Gordon D. *Caudiciform and Pachycaul Succulents*. Mill Valley, CA: Strawberry Press, 1987.

Sajeva, Maurizo, and Mariangela Costanza. *Succulents, the Illustrated Dictionary*. Portland, OR: Timber Press, 1994.

Sunset Books. *Western Garden Book*. Menlo Park, CA: Lane Publishers, 1997.

Thomson, Mildred L., and Edward J. Thomson. *Begonias*. New York: Times Books, 1998.

PLANT INDEX

Adenium obesum

Adiantum raddianum 'Sea Foam'

Adromischus cristatus

Aechmea chantinii 'Dwarf'

Aeranges hybrid

African violet (see *Sainpaulia*)

Agave stricta

Aglaomorpha species

Aglaonema 'Silver Queen'

Aglaonema species

airplane plant (see *Chlorophytum*)

Alocasia x amazonica

Alocasia 'Black Velvet'

Aloe haworthioides

Aloe humilis

Aloe parvula

Aloe species

American pitcher plant

Angraecum didieri

Angraecum Longiscott

Angranthes Grandalena

Anthurium andraeanum 'Dwarf'

Araceae

aralia family

Araliaceae

areca palm (see *Chrysalidocarpus lutecens*)

Arum family

asparagus fern (see *Asparagus setaceus*)

Asparagus setaceus

Aspidistra elatior 'Milky Way'

Asplenium nidus 'Curly'

bamboo palms (see *Chamaedorea*)

Beaucarnea recurvata

Begonia 'Boston Blackie'

Begonia 'Brown Swirl'

Begonia 'Dewdrop'

begonia family

Begonia 'Granada'

Begonia 'Guy Savard'

Begonia 'Kismet'

Begonia 'La Paloma'

Begonia variety

Begoniaceae

Billbergia 'Fantasia'

Billbergia hybrid

bladderwort (see *Utricularia*)

Boston fern (see *Nephrolepis*)

Brassaia arboricola 'Dwarf'

Brassaia arboricola 'Variegated Dwarf'

Brassavola nodosa

Bromeliaceae

bromeliad family

butterfly palm (see *Chrysalidocarpus lutecens*)

butterwort (see *Pinguicola*)

Cactceae

cactus family

Calathea makoyana

carnivorous plants

Cephalotus follicularis

Ceropegia woodii

chainlink rhipsalis (see *Rhipsalis paradoxa*)

Chamaedorea

Chamaedorea erumpens

Chamaedorea seifrizii

Chlorophytum bichetii

Chlorophytum comosum 'Mandaianum'

Cobra pitcher (see *Darlingtonia californica*)

Codonanthe crassifolia

coontie (see *Zamia floridana*)

Crassula argentea

Crassula argentea 'Golem'

Crassula cornuta

Crassula marnieriana

Crassula perforata

crown of thorns (see *Euphorbia splendens*)

Cryptanthus beuckeri

Cryptanthus fosterianus

Cryptanthus hybrid

cycad family

Cycadaceae

Cycas

Cycas revoluta

Davallia species

Dendrobium hybrid

Dieffenbachia

Dionaea

Dracaena

Dracaena fragrans

Dracaena marginata

Dracula vampira 'Nosferatu'

Drosera

Drynaria species

earth star (see *Cryptanthus*)

Echeveria 'Alpine Rose'

Echeveria hybrid

Euphorbia caput-medusae

Euphorbia lactea 'Cristata'

Euphorbia species

Euphorbia splendens

Euphorbia stenoclada

Euphorbia tirucalli

Euphorbia tortirama

Euphorbia trigona

fake fig

fake moss

Faucaria tuberculosa

Ferns (see *Adiantum, Aglaomorpha, Asplenium, Davallia, Drynaria, Humata, Microsorum, Platycerium, Pyrrosia*)

Ficus fakius (fake fig)

Ficus pumila 'Quercifolia'

Ficus pumila 'Variegata'

Fig (see *Ficus*)

Gastworthia hybrid

Geranium hybrid

Gesneriaceae

gesneriad family

Gibasis geniculata (see *Tradescantia multiflora*)

Gypsophila paniculata

Haemaria discolor

hare's-foot fern (see *Davallia* or *Humata*)

Hatiora salicornioides

Haworthia fasciata

Haworthia papillosa

Haworthia xiphiophylla

Humata species

jade plant (see *Crassula argentea*)

jewel orchid (see *Haemaria*)

lady of the night orchid (see *Brassavola nodosa*)

Lady of the night orchid (see *Brassavola nodosa*)

lady palms (see *Rhapis*)

Liliaceae

lily family

Mammillaria fragilis
Marantaceae
Microsorum punctatum
Microsorum punctatum 'Cristatum Compactum'
Microsorum punctatum 'Cristatum Dwarf'
Miltonia
Miltonidium Cleo's Pride
Ming aralia (see *Polyscias fruticosa*)
Monadium stapelloides
Mossus fakius (fake moss)
moth orchid (see *Phalaenopsis*)

Neoregelia hybrid
Neoregelia marmorata
Neoregelia tigrina
Nepenthes ampullaria
Nepenthes gracilis
Nepenthes hybrid
Nephrolepis exaltata 'Dallas'

Odontoglossum
old man's beard (see *Rhipsalis capilliformis*)
Oncidium
Opuntia
Opuntia 'Golem'
orchid family
Orchidaceae

Pachypodium lamerei
palm family
Palmae
Paphiopedilum barbigerum
Paphiopedilum concolor x *P.* Pinocchio
Paphiopedilum Maudiae 'Magnificum'
Paphiopedilum Ron Williamson
Paphiopedilum sukhakulii
parlor palm (see *Chrysalidocarpus lutecens*)
peacock moss (see *Selaginella wildenovii*)
peacock plant (see *Calathea*)
Pedilanthus species
Peperomia caperata 'Emerald Ripple'
peperomia family
Peperomiaceae
Phalaenopsis hybrid
Philodendron
Pinguicola moranensis
pitcher plant (see *Darlingtonia, Heliamphora, Nepenthes,* and *Sarracenia*)
Platycerium bifurcatum 'Dwarf'
Platycerium elephantotis
Platycerium ellisii
Platycerium grande

pleurothallid orchids (see *Dracula*)
Polyscias fruticosa 'Dwarf'
pony tail palm (Beaucarnea recurvata)
prayer plant family
Psilotum nudum
Pyrrosia lingua 'Obaki'

Restrepia striata
resurrection fern (see *Selaginella lepidophylla*)
Rhapis excelsea
Rhipsalis capilliformis
Rhipsalis paradoxa
Rhipsalis teres
Rhombophyllum dolabriforme

Sago palm (see *Cycas revoluta*)
Saintpaulia hybrid
Sansevieria
Sarracenia
Schefflera (see *Brassaia*)
Sedum spathulifolium 'Cape Blanco'
Selaginella kraussiana 'Aurea'
Selaginella lepidophylla
Selaginella pallescens
Selaginella species
Selaginella uncinata
Selaginella wildenovii

Selaginellacea
Sempervivum 'Alpine Rose'
Senecio descoingsii
Senecio haworthii
Senecio scaposus
Seyrigia humbertii
slipper orchid (see *Paphiopedilum*)
Spanish moss (see *Tillandsia usneoides*)
Spathiphyllum
spike moss (see *Selaginella*)
spikemoss family
Streptocarpus hybrid
succulents (see p. ___ for a list of some families)
sun pitcher plant (see *Heliamphora*)
sundew (see *Drosera*)
Syngonium 'Dwarf'

Tacitus bellus
Tillandsia abidida
Tillandsia albida
Tillandsia araujei
Tillandsia argentea
Tillandsia butzii
Tillandsia butzii
Tillandsia caput-medusae
Tillandsia cyanea
Tillandsia filifolia
Tillandsia gemniflora

Tillandsia ionantha
Tillandsia juncea
Tillandsia plumosa
Tillandsia pruinosa
Tillandsia seleriana
Tillandsia streptophylla
Tillandsia usneoides
Tradescantia multiflora
Tylecodon reticulata

Utricularia
Utricularia saundersii

Venus's fly-trap (see Dionaea)
Vriesea 'Polonia'
Vriesea splendens

West Australian pitcher plant (see *Cephalotus follicularis*)
wisk fern (see *Psilotum nudum*)

Zamia
Zamia floridana
Zamia furfuracea
Zamiaceae
Zamioculcas zamiifolia